DISCARD

Social change in a Spanish village

Social Change in a Spanish Village

Aerial view of El Pinar Looking northwestward to the "Pinar Antiguo" forest.

SOCIAL CHANGE IN A SPANISH VILLAGE

Joseph Aceves

SCHENKMAN PUBLISHING COMPANY
CAMBRIDGE, MASSACHUSETTS, USA
AND LONDON, ENGLAND

Copyright © 1971
Schenkman Publishing Company, Inc.
Cambridge, Massachusetts 02138
PRINTED IN THE UNITED STATES OF AMERICA
Library of Congress Catalog Card Number: 74-135342
All rights reserved. This book, or parts thereof, may not be reproduced in any form
without written permission of the publishers.

Preface

UNLESS IT IS to visit relatives or friends, there is little reason for anyone to visit El Pinar. No cathedrals, castles, artistic treasures, or scenic wonders attract the tourist to it. No famous battles were fought there, no great men were born there, and the last time a Spanish chief of state visited the village was in the 13th century . . . and he didn't even stay there all day. Until about 1955, when government sponsored development plans began to be implemented, El Pinar was just another dusty Castillian village steeped in poverty and often misery. But for those interested in social and technological change, El Pinar is important. It was one of the first villages in the country to benefit from programs such as land reform and *Ordenación Rural* which are described in this book.

The average tourist who visits Spain—and 22 million did in 1969—sees little of the life in the small villages except for what glimpses he may get from the window of his bus, train, or automobile. The same can be said about visitors to any country, of course, but Spain to me is not just any country. Anthropologists sometimes refer to the people they have studied as "my people" because of the close ties and friendships that often develop during an extended period of fieldwork. In the case of El Pinar, my ties to the villagers also include ties by blood; many of them really *are* "my people" and represent to me something more than is implied in that cold technical term "informant." While I have tried in every way to be a detached and scientifically rigorous observer of their life, I feel a certain need to describe for others the changes that are affecting their lives in the hope that by understanding the lives of the people in El Pinar, the reader will come to understand, and care about, the lives of millions like them who eke out a bare existence on the dry plains of the Spanish *Meseta*.

This book begins with a description of the village area, the social life and values of the people, and goes on to discuss change programs and their effects on El Pinar and its area. It concludes with a brief analysis of the relationship between values and acceptance or rejection of change. My goal is to introduce the general reader to the problems of rural Spain and to some of the ways these problems are being ameliorated. I make no pretense that this book is a complete ethnography of the village nor that my analysis represents a complete theory of social change. Only a partial account of life in El Pinar is given here; as for my analysis, it represents what I feel is a reasonable argument, based upon data gathered in the field, that seems useful in explaining why the villagers act as they do.

For the benefit of readers interested in expanding their knowledge of Spain, I have appended a brief list of works of interest and importance. Much of the literature on Spain is either so heavily romanticized or politically biased as to be useless in achieving a valid understanding of the country and its people. The suggested readings are, I think, accurate in their descriptions and explanations and well worth reading.

The research and writing of this book would have been impossible without the help of a great many people and organizations. The first period of fieldwork from June 1966 to September 1967 was supported by a grant from the American Universities Research Program of the Agricultural Development Council, Inc. and a Pre-Doctoral Fellowship from the Wenner-Gren Foundation for Anthropological Research, Inc. After a brief visit to Spain during December 1968 and January 1969, I was able to return to El Pinar from June through August 1969 supported by a grant from the Committee on Faculty Grants of the Social Science Research Council.

During the summers of 1966 and 1967, Wilfrid C. Bailey of the University of Georgia was in the field with me and his assistance was most valuable. Whatever merit this book has is due in large part to his efforts. Michael Kenny was in Spain during 1967 and, in addition to being a gracious host, was a valuable source of ideas and criticism. For their ideas, assistance, and encouragement, I thank Charles M. Hudson, Frank Clune, Robert T. Anderson, and Claudio Esteva Fabregat.

Without exception, Spanish authorities were most helpful and hospitable. The Director of *Fundación FOESSA* allowed me to use unpublished data from the Foundation's surveys, and staff members of the *Instituto Nacional de Estadística, Banco Español de Credito, Servicio de Concentración Parcelaria y Ordenación Rural, Promoción Professional Obrera, Servicio de Estensión Agrária,* and *Guardia Civil* all gave unstintingly of their time when asked.

Special thanks are due Dr. Rafael Caldevilla Potente and his wife, Doña Santas, who helped my beleaguered stomach in its unceasing battle with Spanish cooking and whose home was so often a haven of intellectual stimulation. I thank heaven also for people like Don Juan Seco Carrascal and his delightful family whose hospitality can never adequately be repaid.

The people of El Pinar, Leyes, Villa Roman and neighboring villages were magnificent. While most were never quite sure what I was up to, they were always willing to be of assistance. It was a pleasure to live among them and count them as my friends, and I regret the need of maintaining anonymity prohibits my citing their names here.

Thanks are also due David Brokensha and my colleague Ben Wallace for editorial assistance in putting this book together.

My parents, Mary and Paul Aceves, were invaluable sources of information on El Pinar and their ideas, suggestions, and criticisms contributed substantially to my research. Their assistance is just one more thing I am indebted to them for, and my dedication of this book to them is a token payment on that debt.

Table of Contents

Introduction

WE ARE PLEASED to add to the Schenkman Series on Socio-Economic Change this volume by Dr. Joseph Aceves whose study of a changing Castillian village exemplifies most of our aims in this series.

Dr. Aceves has special connections with El Pinar: he is not only an anthropologist studying the village, but also the son of a villager, his father having emigrated from El Pinar to the U.S.A. This double link gives the author a special view, making him keenly aware of the villagers as individuals, while also analysing the modes of institutional change. In addition, Dr. Aceves has a keen sense of both the history and the geography of El Pinar. He shows how present values have been shaped in previous centuries, and how the mediocre soil limits the possibilities of change.

The reader is presented with an overview of the major political, economic and social institutions, in each case supplemented with individual case histories that illuminate the general themes. Much emphasis is placed on the village economy; the author examines in detail the prospects for the pine trees, the basis of the economy, and for the cereals and sugar beets that are also important. He concludes that neither the pines nor the cereal grains are economically attractive, and that, coupled with increased exposure to the "outside world," this leads to an increasing rate of migration, either to the cities of Spain or to France or Germany on a short-term basis. Most younger people wish to leave the village.

Resistance to, and acceptance of, specific changes are considered, Dr. Aceves concluding—in line with similar studies elsewhere—that changes that offer immediate and direct benefits to the individual and his family are likely to be easily accepted. However, if changes involve a long-term contractual relationship with others, such as the establishment of co-operatives—then resistance is likely to occur. Examples of change include diet, introduction of tractors, and new methods of tapping pines.

Two valuable chapters deal with values, with the familiar Mediterranean concepts of honor, shame, the good life, and with a less well known idea of tranquility—"the need for peace and order . . ." that is achieved by avoidance behavior. Some major analyses of peasant values, including Edward Banfield's "amoral familism," and George Foster's "Image of Limited Good," are critically examined in relation to the El Pinar situation. Further, the author deals with "the Arcadian myth" and demonstrates the ambivalence in planning policy, as well as the virtually complete lack of village participation in planning.

This study is critical yet sympathetic: it shows that the views of the villagers are consistent and logical from their assumptions, and that these assumptions are based on time and place. Although writing mainly of one Spanish village, Dr. Aceves is sensitive to the links with the outside world, and to the relation of El Pinar to other villages.

For these reasons, this book, while primarily a detailed study of change in one particular Spanish village, is also relevant for the study of socio-economic change in other villages, and other countries. We found much that was directly comparable to our field experiences in West Africa, Central California and the Phillipines.

DAVID BROKENSHA
BEN J. WALLACE

SOCIAL CHANGE IN A SPANISH VILLAGE

JOSEPH B. ACEVES

Southern Methodist University

FRANCE

ATLANTIC OCEAN

BILBAO

VALLADOLIO

EL PINAR

SEGOVIA

BARCELONA

PORTUGAL

MADRID

SPAIN

MEDITERRANEAN SEA

MALAGA

Map of Spain locating El Pinar

CHAPTER I

Studying El Pinar

Entry

WHEN I ARRIVED in El Pinar, people repeatedly asked why I was there. Invariably, I replied that I was interested in rural development in Spain and had come to observe and to write a book based on my observations. But why, they would persist, would I live in a small village instead of in the more comfortable and stimulating atmosphere of the city? Why not go to Madrid or Valladolid to the universities there and ask the professors who specialized in such things? Again and again I would repeat that wheat did not grow on Madrid's *Gran Via* and that few professors knew how to handle a plow. My place was in El Pinar and its *comarca* (district) because that was where the people who interested me were living. The answer seemed to satisfy their curiosity. The next question was most often phrased as a combination demand and plea: would I tell *the truth* about Spain?

The average Spaniard is sensitive about this matter. He believes that Spain has been unfairly depicted to the world as a backward country in the grip of an iron dictatorship and dominated by a fanatic clergy who still stage *auto de fe's* in the spirit of the Inquisition: this is the heritage of the "Black Legend" about Spain.

In Roquefort, France, I chanced upon an elderly Spanish refugee who had fled to France in 1938 for political reasons. Sitting in a cafe, he told of the hardships of living in a country still foreign to him after almost thirty years' residence. My suggestion that he return to Spain and avail himself of the general amnesty for political exiles was instantly rebuffed. Didn't I know that Spain was gripped by poverty, that governmental tyranny was rife, and that he would certainly be shot if he returned? I gave him an account of what I had seen but it was useless; he had his own version of the truth and believed no other.

The other side of the coin is what could be called the "White Legend," spread by government propagandists and apologists for the Regime. The main theme of this "Legend" is that Spain has, since the 1936-1939 Civil War, avoided the horrors of world war, and achieved a notable improvement in housing and education under the stability and order brought about by the present Regime.

The third edge of the coin, upon which it rolls, is the view of Spain held by the tourists who have flocked there in record numbers since 1960. In 1966 some seventeen million tourists, almost half of them French, visited Spain; in 1969 the number reached 22 million. The tourists' truth, which may as well be called the "Golden Legend" stems from an appreciation for low prices, good hotels, sun, seashore, art treasures, and that congeries of material and social artifacts known as *típico* (the typical). Their impressions of Spain are frequently a blend of "Carmen," flamenco music and dance, bullfights, castles, *vino*, and fiestas served up by a hospitable populace of gay peasant types and/or sophisticated Latins out of Cervantes by Don Juan Tenorio. Thus the holiday visitor takes home an impression of Spain which I call "ersatz Andalus"—a grossly exaggerated version of coastal Andalusion life. There seems to be general agreement that the Spanish people are a wonderful lot even if the Castillian peasant is almost oriental in his frozen dignity and inscrutability. This latter can readily be "proven" by reading the work of writers such as V.S. Pritchett, and Ernest Hemingway.

Each of the above "legends" has a certain validity to it. In answer to the plea for truth, all I could reply was that I would make my observations with an open mind. In essence, my answer to my hosts was that I would record the truth as the people said *they* saw it before I made any attempt at analysis, and would refrain from the role of social critic.

The basic method used was participant-observation: I lived in the village continually and became accepted by the people as a regular resident. Once they were accustomed to me, it was easy to join in the local activities, converse with the people, observe their actions, and on many occasions, join in with some of the work.

My arrival in El Pinar was not unanticipated; indeed, for some of the people it was a major event. My father was born in El Pinar and grew up there prior to his emigration to the United States in 1921. My mother, born in the United States of non-Spanish parents, first visited the village in 1932 and had returned on many other visits. I had spent five months in El Pinar during 1949 and maintained a sporadic correspondence with relatives there. My father, of course, had kept in frequent touch with his family and friends. The presence of kin in the village was helpful in establishing an immediate rapport, as was the presence of many old friends. But, once the rapport had been established, the kin group proved to be neither a special help nor hindrance in study; I was able to meet and develop friendships with a large number of people on my own initiative.

My interests extended to other villages in the *comarca* and it was no hard task to interview and observe in these villages where I was unknown. If people see you frequently and if you are friendly and pose no threat to them, usually it is a simple matter to gain acceptance. After two months I was a familiar sight and my coming and going aroused no particular comment.

To my face I was called by my name—in Spanish form, of course—and to others I was *el Americano*. In a community where practically everybody has a nickname and where last names are usually little used, this label was both descriptive and convenient as well as non-malevolent.

Statements that I was studying rural development were generally accepted although my exact role in the village seldom became clear. Few people in any community have precise ideas of what anthropologists do. Sometimes I was asked if I was measuring heads. Others wanted to know if I considered the Spaniards to be primitive people like "those in Africa" since anthropologists supposedly study primitives exclusively.

The complexity of the problem and the size of the village made it impractical to use just one key informant, nor did I wish to trust data obtained from only one or two people. Therefore, I sought data from many informants and usually tried to get data from people well versed in a particular occupational specialty, or who held a particular social position. Whenever possible, I asked at least two persons about the same phenomenon, but never in such a way as to imply that I did not trust what someone had told me. Whenever in doubt I would check with several people whose judgement I trusted. It was rare that I ever felt that someone was deliberately misleading me or lying. Often a person would overstate or understate a situation, but I am confident that information was always offered in good faith and represented what the person felt to be the truth.

There is much intra-familial and inter-personal rivalry in the village as well as the usual gossip and backbiting. One task was to make sure that I knew at least the major feuds and cases of which people were not on speaking terms. I made it clear that I was neutral and that I wanted to be on good terms with everybody; all agreed that it was a wise course of action, and most of the time it presented no difficulty.

One of the ways to meet people in Spain (as elsewhere) is to be "passed along" from one person to another. Everyone seems to have a relative who can help, or who knows someone who in turn knows someone else with the needed information. For example, Manolito, about fifteen years old, was crossing a street in Segovia when he was run down by a youth on a motorcycle. The police took him to a first aid station and later to the hospital where he spent six weeks; the driver was questioned and released.

When I heard of the accident, I drove to the hospital in Segovia with Manolito's uncle Julian. After ascertaining that the boy was doing well, we then decided to find out who the motorcycle driver was; Manolito had forgotten his name. What followed was typical behavior: Julian had a friend in the *Guardia Civil,* who had served with him in the Army, and who would be helpful at the police station although *Guardia Civil* officers have no direct jurisdiction in the city. Juan, the friend, appeared and we went to the police station where we were told that the documents on the case had been sent to the municipal court. My suggestion that we go directly to the court was rejected by both men on the grounds that we knew nobody there to help us. Then followed a day and a half of investigation; we talked to the agency that sold the motorcycle of the make that hit Manolito; the cycle shop owner referred us to a friend who sold the insurance and who might remember the boy as a customer. In the meanwhile, everybody tried vainly to find someone who had influence at the court. The one contact we could locate, the friend of a son-in-law of a refinery owner in El Pinar, was in Madrid. Finally, the three of us being near the Courthouse, I dragged them in and asked the clerk if he had records of the accident. He, being satisfied that we had a right to know, simply checked the records and told us the driver's name, address, and insurance policy number. Julian and Juan were almost stupefied at getting the information in this way—I had violated the norms appropriate to the situation but did get the desired results. I also met a lot of people that normally I would not have encountered.

In these kinds of situations the researcher should go along with the time consuming process of being passed on because he may meet somebody along the way who proves to be of assistance in other areas of interest.

Formal interviews were few and were usually restricted to professional people such as physicians, school teachers, Agricultural Extension agents, and some government officials. Much of the conversation took place in the local bars and was informal in nature; sometimes it was just small talk, other times a topic of special interest to me would arise and I would try to keep the conversation going and elicit information.

It was rare to have a scheduled interview in any of the villages; one could not rush things too much and it was possible to wait for opportunities to bring up topics at the right moment. Rather than create social situations, I felt it wiser to fit into the normal pattern of life and to discuss what the people discussed rather than always bringing up things of special interest to me but not necessarily to them.

The question of validity always arises in studies of this type, and, concerned over the validity of my observations and conclusions, I used the technique of having several reliable informants as a review panel for my ideas. This involved discussing tentative conclusions and new ideas with them to see if these were reasonable. The members of this group were a diverse lot; a schoolteacher, a physician, a receptionist in a hotel, and others who were objective about their own culture and able to give honest appraisals.

I have used pseudonyms for all persons mentioned in this report as well as for the villages involved in the study. Some dates and figures have been changed to maintain the anonymity of people and places.

A brief history

The first record of El Pinar is an Eighth century document in the Cathedral archives in Segovia noting that the place was a gathering place for shepherds. A dispute between Villa Roman and Los Encierros arose over ownership of the spot and Alfonxo X., "The Learned," was forced to go to the site and settle the argument between the two powerful contending Villas. He divided the lands, giving half to Villa Roman and half to Los Encierros, and thus El Pinar was divided into two *barrios* (neighborhoods), each belonging to a different owner. This occurred on Friday, November 8, 1258. The dividing line was a street known to this day as the *Calle de la Raya* . . . the street of the boundary line.

Details of life in El Pinar's *barrios* are scarce but it is possible to extrapolate from what is known about life in Villa Roman, the closest of two ruling Villas. A Royal Questionaire of 1759 and the answers to its forty questions is on file in El Pinar and gives some data about the *barrio de Los Encierros*. That *barrio* was owned by the Dukes of Albuquerque with the Crown owning no land. The lands were described as being of "medium quality," and the main crops were cereal grains, barley, and wheat. The pay of an agriculture worker was described, vaguely, as depending upon what he did. There was a church, one parish priest, a tavern-inn and the same agricultural characteristics. It is reasonable to infer that the social life was no different in one *barrio* than in the other; political boundaries, especially a three meter wide street, are not necessarily social boundaries. A judicious estimate would place the combined population at about 250 inhabitant in 1760.

The El Pinar area lived through one of its most important crises during the War of Independence fought against France. On 2 December 1808, French forces under General Milhaud took Villa Roman; despite the General's assurances, the troops sacked the town, committing various acts of vandalism, robbery and rape. The villagers responded violently:

. . . inspired by their patriotic ardor, a group of peasants with no more than their working tools for arms attacked a French patrol a few days later; precisely on the same day that the *Junta Central* decreed the formation of the famous bands of *guerrillas* which so effectively contributed to the weakening and demoralization of the arrogant armies of Napoleon.

The guerrillas of Villa Roman and its lands grew in number rapidly. Comprised of rude men who knew the extensive pine forests of the area, they fought unceasingly and with hardly any rest inasmuch as the illustrious Villa was an obligatory stopping point on the route from Valladolid to Segovia, and a postal station for the mail couriers of the foreign King. (Gonzales Casanova, 1948)

Lord Wellington passed through Villa Roman and made it his field headquarters for several weeks during the campaign. During this period and until the war's end in 1814, an English garrison was kept in the area.

In 1849 El Pinar had nearly 500 inhabitants living in 180 houses which were distributed about various streets and plazas. The existence of two churches and two jails testify to the former *barrio* division. Shortly afterward, the church in the *barrio de Los Encierros* was closed and its congregation merged with the Villa Roman *barrio's*. The resin industry was flourishing. There was one schoolteacher, mail arrived three times a week, and the roads were in "good" condition.

In 1855 El Pinar had 955 inhabitants and 287 houses. The historical data indicate that there was little notable about the houses or municipal edifices beyond the fact they were situated on dirty streets and plazas where the paving—where it existed—was badly done. Those conditions were prevalent throughout Spanish pueblos of that time; even today it is not uncommon in the rural areas. The single school of 1849 had been expanded to two schools, the sexes being segregated, as is still Spanish custom, and there were two school masters.

The El Pinar area's normal tranquility was interrupted by the Carlist Wars in the late Nineteenth Century—wars that affected the area little—and by the Spanish American War in which several of the villagers saw active duty in Cuba. The political travails that periodically engulfed Madrid and the urban centers and the turbulent Basque, Catalan, and Andalusian areas touched the village only lightly. Governments, Kings, and Ministers came and went, but the daily life of El Pinar and other obscure *pueblos* continued in its inexorable way. The Civil War of 1936-1939 was the next major crisis for the area.

El Pinar never suffered bombardments nor were any major military actions fought within its boundaries. The nearest front was that of the Guadarrama Mountains, some 50 kilometers away. Yet, no one really escaped the war and it became the great temporal divide for those old enough to remember it. For the citizens of El Pinar, as well as for most Spaniards, history is divided into two periods; before the War and after it.

The vast majority of the people in the *comarca* were pro-Franco and against the "Reds," as the Republican forces were known. The area itself was relatively secure; the horrors of war came not in vast battles but in the midnight knock upon the door of some unsuspecting peasant by a partisan band who took him off, tried him summarily, and imprisoned him or shot him to death. A man was denounced by people from his own village, but it was always men from another village who seized him and performed the execution. The same pattern was generally true in both the Nationalist and the Republican areas. Sometimes the trial would be held in another place and the execution carried out there; sometimes the man was taken out and, without being allowed even to say goodbye to his wife and children, was shot to death as his family watched, unable to do or say anything.

There is a hill near the hamlet of La Mesita, midway between El Pinar and Segovia that symbolizes the horror of civil war as it affected the *comarca*. Rufino was a 35-year-old *resinero,* and average sort of man with no great wealth or talent. He was denounced by an unknown villager for reasons he never knew. It could be that he had

some land that another man coveted, perhaps his irregular attendance at Mass was regarded as a crime, no one to this day knows or is
willing to say. Condemned to death, at a drumhead court-martial, he
and several others from the area were driven to La Mesita and, in the
bleak dawn of a Castillian winter day, given shovels and ordered to
dig their own graves. The others dawdled, they were in no hurry to
die; Rufino in his anger dug the shallow grave, spat in it, and sat down
cursing to smoke a cigarette.

As the machine-gun was being tested by the firing squad, a Regular Army officer chanced by in a truck. Attracted by the firing, he
stopped to investigate and recognized Rufino. The officer was from the
comarca and knew the condemned man and his family. "My God,
why are you here?", was his question. Rufino could only curse and say
that he didn't know. Resigned to death, he neither wept nor cried as
did many but rather cursed and urged the firing squad to get on with
it. The officer sought out the partisan leader and, after much argument and some threats, took Rufino off with him on the pretext that
he was wanted for further interrogation. Both men heard the machine
gun chattering as the truck drove off. Once near the Guadarrama
Mountains, the officer turned him loose with the advice that he seek
security in the "Red" zone until after the war. He also told Rufino
that he would kill him if he ever saw him again since, by his actions,
the officer had been guilty of an unpardonable treachery.

When Regular Army units assumed control of the area, the random
killings stopped and some type of due process took place. But neither
the victors nor the vanquished in a civil war have much to rejoice
about or to glory in. 1940 and 1941 were the "years of hunger"; even
bread was virtually unobtainable since the government requisitioned
all the wheat for use in feeding the cities. Farmers hid small quan-
tities of grain in double walls built into houses and barns; carts covered with tarpaulins made midnight trips through the woods to secret
mills where grain could be ground into flour, and even the *Guardia
Civil* managed to look the other way most of the time so as not to have
to enforce the law. It took a long post-war period for El Pinar—and all
of Spain—to recover from the ravages of the civil war and achieve
some measure of prosperity.

In 1949, when I lived in El Pinar for five months, it was then little
more than another adobe village, although the population of approximately 1,700 made it still one of the largest villages in the Province,
and its income from pine leases made it one of the richer villages. The
streets were unpaved except for a rough concrete slab in the Plaza

which abutted the handball court. There was no running water in the houses and people got drinking water from a number of wells and hydrants scattered about the village. Flies and fleas were abundant and, although the insides of the houses were neat and clean, the streets were strewn with animal manure and miscellaneous refuse. These conditions are noted in an official document which points out the existence of:

. . . primitive shacks clustered in narrow and twisting streets where the filth and excrement of both people and animals is the major characteristic.

To say that changes have taken place between 1949 and 1969 would be the grossest of understatements. The changes are best symbolized by the cats. Driving into the village in June 1966 it was constantly necessary to step on the brakes to avoid hitting cats. These were alley cats of no discernible breed and they were all fat and healthy looking. I did not think too much about it until some weeks later when I got to reminiscing with an old friend about 1949. In that era about all we ever ate was a *cocido* (stew) made from potatoes, garbanzos, and rabbit meat. Every home had its corral and rabbit hutch and rabbit meat was a common staple diet item. In 1966, nobody was eating rabbits and, they explained, the rabbits had all died from a disease several years ago anyway. Maybe I saw a cat run across the street or perhaps something else triggered my thoughts because I commented to my friends that I distinctly remembered that there were only a few cats in El Pinar in 1949 and those were so wild and wary that no one could get near them. At that point, it dawned upon me that cats are edible. A comment to that effect brought an awkward silence and then a general burst of laughter from the assembled men. "When you skin a cat and a rabbit, who can tell the difference?", was one's comment and my suspicions were then confirmed about what really went into some of that *cocido*. The difference between rabbit (and cat) on the table in 1949 and chicken and lamb chops in 1966 is one measure of how El Pinar has changed for the better.

Why El Pinar?

Prior knowledge of the area made the choice of El Pinar convenient and attractive to me, but its situation as a representative village and the fact that it is one of the first villages to have benefitted from the *Ordenación Rural* program made it important for the purposes of this study. Every village has some unique characteristic, some peculiarity of its own, not exhibited elsewhere, at least not to the same degree. This is not important for El Pinar's people are in no significant way different from those of other villages of the *comarca,* the Province, or the wider region. El Pinar provides a base from which we may safely generalize with reference to other villages in the region.

Spain is a country of small villages; less than 73.5% of its 9,202 incorporated municipalities have populations exceeding 2,000. This settlement pattern is most notable in the Two Castilles, Leon, the interior of Galicia, and parts of Aragon and Extremadura. Comprising 34.3% of the total land area of Spain, the area cited has 25.4% of the Spanish population and 42% of all incorporated municipalities. However, by excluding major cities such as Madrid, Valladolid, and Leon, we find that the remaining population in this vast area does not exceed 15% of the national total. The population density of the rural areas is 60.45 persons per square mile compared to the overall national mean of 155.92. Furthermore, the rural areas are losing population as people move from rural areas to cities. Segovia Province in 1970 has less inhabitants than in 1940 and decreasing population is noted in the neighboring provinces of Avila and Soria.

Sociologists at the *Fundación FOESSA,* a research branch of *Caritas Española*—Spanish Catholic Charities—divided the nation into "homogeneous social units" (more properly, homogeneous socio-economic units) which ignored traditional diocesan, provincial, or regional boundaries. El Pinar is located in a "Zonal Type" composed of 98 such units which together can be treated as an area of marked socio-economic homogeneity. In this area live approximately one-quarter of the rural Spanish population and only 11% of the nation's urban population. The predominant economic activity is agriculture practised by self-employed farm owners or renters and the way of life is almost completely rural.

The general nature of the area is summed up by *FOESSA* sociologists as being characterized by *minifundio* in agriculture with a typically rural socio-cultural social structure including a rigid traditionalism which impedes the adoption of favorable attitudes toward innovation and, as a consequence, of development. The area shows a marked population is employed in agriculture with a low percentage of temporary day laborers. About one-sixth of the families are insufficiently fed. Relatively good medical and pharmacy services are available. Illiteracy is low in most of the area although opportunities for secondary and higher education are scarce. There is almost no housing shortage, but quality housing is lacking and poor paving, sewerage disposal systems, and water supply is common. About half of the area's villages are fully served by electric power lines, and telephone service is generally available in almost all villages.[1]

Based upon comparisons of various statistical data and upon direct observation of much of the area described above, El Pinar can be described as being one of the "better" villages of the area. That is, it has more of the tangible signs of development, *e.g.*, paved streets, running water, a good school, than do most villages. This is largely due to its relatively greater municipal wealth as well as to its having been selected by the Provincial government for development in 1955, much earlier than most of the other 3,837 municipalities in the area. However, in general the people and the social structure of El Pinar are not significantly different from those found elsewhere in the *comarca*, the Province, or the wider area outlined by the *FOESSA* sociologists.

---

[1] The detailed methodology, and data on the various units can be found in Caritas Española, 1965, vol. 1.

CHAPTER II

The Village

Location And Communications

EL PINAR IS LOCATED in the west-central part of the Province of Segovia. Situated on the northern *Meseta* (plateau) of the Iberian peninsula at a latitude approximating that of Omaha, Nebraska (41° 5′ North), the general terrain features look much like the American Plains.

It is not especially difficult to reach El Pinar; the *pueblo*[1] has good communications with the rest of Spain. From Madrid a modern road leads north toward Villalba and across the Sierra de Guadarrama to Segovia, capital city of the Province of the same name. From Segovia the road, a two lane paved road leads out past the Alcazar castle onto the gentle rolling Castillian plain and passes through grain fields until it reaches the extensive pine forest from which El Pinar derives its name and most of its wealth. By automobile, it is about a two and one-half hour ride from Madrid; by bus or train it takes about five hours with good connections.

The Mediterraneo-Continental climate is harsh; summers are hot and winters long and cold. Spring and Fall tend to be brief. In the summer, temperatures in the sun regularly exceed 100°F; the ground cracks in the heat and plants wither. While snow is rare on the plain,

---

[1] *Pueblo* means both a population unit such as a village or town or the people of that place; the intended usage is derived from the context. A third meaning is that of "hick" or "country bumpkin" and may be applied to either a settlement or a person or people. It is possible to make further distinguish and classify *pueblos* by size or settlement types such as *aldeas* (hamlets), etc., but these distinctions are rarely used by the people who generally make a distinction only between *ciudad* (city) and *pueblo*.

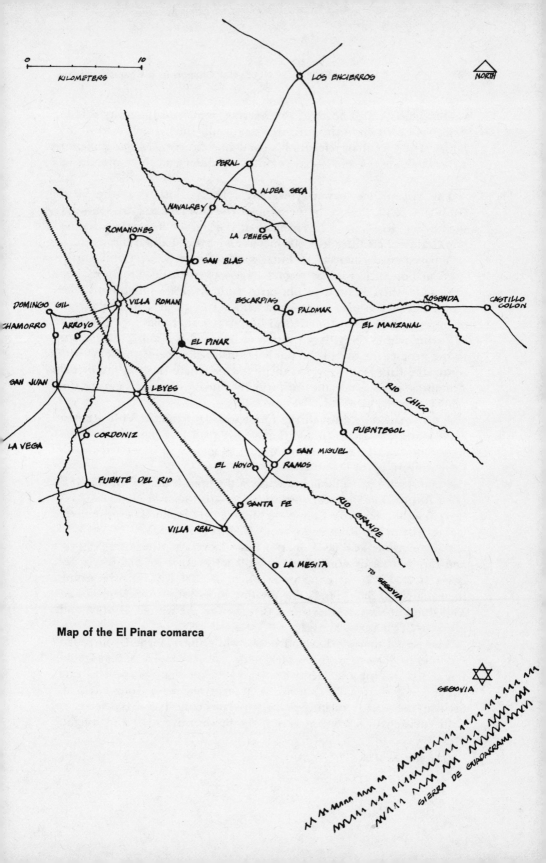

Map of the El Pinar comarca

winter temperatures hover at the freezing point and the misty drizzle
that passes for rain in this arid area soon chills the hardiest man to his
bones. The Castillian refers to his climate as *"nueve meses de invierno
y tres meses de infierno"*—nine months of winter and three months of
hell.

The village lies between two rivers known locally as the "Rio
Grande"—ironically, for in the summer the flow falls to a trickle—and
the smaller "Rio Chico." It is situated on the high bluffs overlooking the
Rio Grande at an altitude of 805 meters above the Mediterranean Sea.

A paved road connects El Pinar southward to Segovia and northward to Los Encierros, the second largest town in the Province after
the capital city. From Los Encierros with its 6,000 inhabitants, the
road continues to the city of Valladolid. At El Pinar a road branches
off toward the East to the Madrid-Burgos national highway. The lack
of paving within the village portion of the road is a source of concern
to the people; the size of the pot-holes inspired some of the local wits
to ask the City Hall to widen them and designate them as municipal
swimming pools, since they are usually filled with water during the
rainy season.

A dirt road runs through the forest westward toward Villa Roman
eight kilometers away. In addition, a dirt road branches off from the
Turegano road leading to San Miguel, Ramos, and other *pueblos* to
the southeast.

Train service is available in Leyes via the branch line of the RENFE
(*Red National de Ferrocarriles Españoles*—the Spanish National Rail-
way) line that runs from Segovia to Medina del Campo. There are three
trains daily to and from Segovia and Medina del Campo.

Each morning at 8:00 A.M. two buses leave the village for Segovia
and one bus heads northward to Valladolid. Another bus leaves Segovia at 1:30 P.M. arriving in El Pinar at 3:00 P.M. and returning
immediately to the capital. The evening buses leave from Segovia and
Valladolid at six in the evening (five during the winter months) and
arrive in El Pinar two hours later.

These English-made Leyland buses, while uncomfortable on rough
roads and unheated in the winter, make possible journeys that would
have been unthinkable twenty-five years ago. For eighty-six pesetas[2] one
could journey from the *pueblo* to Madrid one way. Round trip to
Segovia, the most frequently made trip, costs only sixty-five pesetas.

In addition to passenger service, the busses carry mail and freight.

[2] 70 pesetas = $1.00.

For a small tip, bus drivers run errands in the cities, deliver messages to people in other villages on the route, and perform other small useful services. The drivers are also a good source of information as to what is going on in villages along their route. This phenomenon is by no means restricted to El Pinar or to Spain; indeed, it is commonplace throughout rural areas in Europe and elsewhere in the world.

The first automobile appeared in El Pinar in 1908. In 1969 there were forty-five private automobiles, thirty-eight motorcycles, thirty-two trucks and three Land Rovers registered in the village. Privately owned automobiles are still a luxury in Spain, most of the vehicles belonging to rich business owners or professionals such as the doctor. Most people ride bicycles or simply walk; farmers use mule or donkey drawn carts when going to their fields. Riding horses are rarely owned or used.

In addition to rail and vehicular connections, El Pinar is linked to the rest of Spain by a very efficient mail service. Mail arrives daily on the train that stops at Leyes and is brought by a motorcycle carrier to the Post Office in El Pinar where it is delivered to the houses each morning; the late mail arrives on the evening bus from Segovia. On an average day, the village receives about 150 pieces of mail.

Telephone service is less efficient. There were eighty-four telephones in homes and offices in 1969, plus a public telephone at the switchboard located in the City Hall. Since the switchboard capacity was only eighty-four lines, no new service could be installed. Calls into and out of the village are routed through Leyes and a call may take several hours to complete since El Pinar shares three trunk lines with several other villages and often only one call at a time is possible.

Completing the linkage with the "outside," almost every home has a radio receiver and about forty homes have television sets as do all of the thirteen bars. Television is a novelty, the first set arriving in the village in 1961. The number of sets indicates a number of relatively prosperous families; a TV receiver cost about 20,000 pesetas, which can be more than a third of the family's annual income.

Copies of the Madrid daily newspaper, *Arriba*, come in on the evening bus and are hawked through the streets by a band of small boys. In addition, about thirty persons in the village subscribe to *El Adelantado de Segovia*, the capital city news daily. Magazines of the pulp romance type are sold in a kiosk on the Plaza, mostly to young girls.

Considering the entire communications network in its fullest meaning, El Pinar can no way be considered an isolated community.

While most of the people travel infrequently, they are exposed to news from the outside and most have been at least as far as Segovia.

The Village Setting

Except for its paved streets, street lighting, and such amenities as a sewage collection system and piped running water in the homes, El Pinar's physical structure is little different from most Castillian villages.

The center of village life is the main Plaza with the church at one end and the City Hall at the other. Most of the shops and bars are located in the Plaza area, either on the Plaza itself or on one of the main streets leading off it. The older village core area still retains the small and twisting street pattern; the new *barrio* opened in 1951 has a more modern appearance. This *barrio,* known simply as *el barrio nuevo,* consists of sixty houses set along wide straight streets, and two small plazas. Most of the houses were built with the aid of government loans amortizable over a forty year period and guaranteed by the Housing Ministry.

El Pinar's industry, mostly resin refineries and saw-mills, is located at one edge of town along the El Manzanal road, although one refinery and a small brickyard are located on the road to Los Encierros.

The town itself is compact, buildings are set side by side and one may walk the length of the village in ten minutes. The municipal boundaries enclose approximately 65 square kilometers, but the village—as is typical in much of Europe—is surrounded by the farm plots and forest, and the farmers and *resineros* go out to their work daily on foot, by wagon, or on their bicycles.

Off the Plaza is the Post Office building which also houses the office of the *Hermandad,* the farmer's "brotherhood". The arrangement is convenient for the Postal Agent who doubles as Secretary of the *Hermandad.* The building itself was the former headquarters of the *Frente de Juventudes* in the village; this national government sponsored youth organization is known now as the *Organización Juvenil Española* and is housed in a new building in the *barrio nuevo.* The old handball court on the Plaza was torn down and replaced by a new one in the *barrio nuevo* during the 1950's.

Women wash their clothes at one of two municipal wash houses. Near the main industrial area is the municipal slaughterhouse where animals are slaughtered under veterinary inspection. In 1963, the village opened a new out-patient clinic off the Plaza; here the resident physician and the *practicante* (a combination male nurse, midwife, and medical technician) hold daily office hours. The clinic is well equipped to handle emergencies if they should arise; the nearest hospital facilities are in Segovia, to which serious cases can be taken by car or ambulance in less than an hour's time.

The interior of the City Hall was remodeled in the 1950's and boasts an elegant *Salon* where the monthly Council meetings are held. It also includes a suite of offices for officials and three apartments for housing the Municipal Secretary and his family, and the families of a schoolteacher and the veterinarian.

The old school was located on the first floor of the City Hall, but in August, 1966 a new school was dedicated by the Provincial Civil Governor. Located away from the village center, this new edifice cost some 4,500,00 pesetas to construct. In addition to spacious classrooms it has central heating, washrooms, and a dining hall. The old classrooms in the City Hall were used for storage and for miscellaneous purposes once the new school opened for use in 1967. During 1969, 308 students (140 boys and 168 girls) were enrolled in Primary School, and 48 students (30 boys and 18 girls) were enrolled in Secondary level courses.

The most immediately visible sign of modernization in El Pinar is the water tower. Completed in 1962, the tower and its pumping facility on the Rio Grande supply most of the village's water supply, although the older pumping station in the hills north of the village is still tied into the water distribution system. There is an adequate supply of pure clear water for domestic and industrial use. Village officials plan to double the capacity of the pumping station to provide more water for irrigation, and some steps had been taken toward this end during 1969.

Public health measures have helped change the village. A number of small ponds on the edge of the village were dried up and a fertile source of mosquitos was eliminated. Although many draft animals such as mules and burros are still kept in the household corral, there is a trend toward keeping them in corrals on the edge of the village away from the housing area. These practices, plus the use of insecticide, have sharply reduced the once thriving insect population, especially fleas and flies.

Notably lacking is a garbage dump. Until recent years the problem had not existed; there had been nothing to throw away. This was literally true; people saved old cans, bottles, string, and anything else of potential use. Garbage and waste food were fed to the

family pig. While there is a recognized waste removal problem in El
Pinar, the streets are kept swept clean. The village sporadically employs a street sweeper, although most of his efforts seem to concentrate on the center of the village. This problem attests to the
village's increasing prosperity.

Most of the houses, practically 99%, have electricity and over 85%
have running water. El Pinar first received electricity in 1911, but
widespread use of electric appliances is a very recent phenomenon.
Power failures are frequent during thunderstorms, high winds (and
often low winds), and when some ancient piece of equipment burns
out. The power system is owned and operated by the village's leading resin processor as one of his many enterprises, but it is tied in to
a region-wide power grid that receives its electricity from hydroelectric generators on the Duero River. Electricity is cheap, as is the
water. Water is furnished by the village at a cost of 8 pesetas a month
for the minimum usage; few people use more than this.

The modernization of much of El Pinar has come about through a
Plan de Ordenación drawn up in 1955 by provincial authorities.
This is a zoning plan as well as a fifty year growth plan which sets
up guidelines for village expansion. Most of the villagers are not
aware of its existence, but the municipal authorities try to follow it,
although not always with great success. One of the most successful
changes inspired by the Plan has been the street straightening project. A number of streets were straightened after the village bought
old houses and tore them down. The little plaza by Tio Ventura's
house was, for example, eliminated by the tearing down of some
houses and extending the streets and sidewalks to form a normal
street interchange. Most of the streets were paved between 1955 and
1960 by using concrete over a crushed stone base. The Plaza was completely paved, an ornamental fountain and little shade trees installed, and stone benches placed for the people to use. All new houses
must follow a setback rule and must be in the proper alignment with
the street and with other houses.

Few of the houses in El Pinar are over 100 years old and the majority
of the older housing has been repaired in the last fifteen years. There
are no slums in El Pinar nor is any area considered to be socially superior to any other. Rich and poor, laborer and professional, live side by
side, though the former have better houses than the latter. This is
usual in the *comarca* but not universal in Spain.[3]

---

[3] *cf.* Lison-Tolesano, 1966 for an account of social segregation in an Aragon village.

There are about 570 houses in the village, of which 20% are un-occupied or in non-residential use. Since 1960, an average of 8 houses a year have been built, but most of these are designed to replace older housing which is torn down once the new house is completed. About 90% of the present housing is owner occupied; few people rent houses. Schoolteachers and certain municipal officials must be provided housing by the village as part of their pay. In the case of the *Guardia Civil,* the *Cuartel* building acts as a combination headquarters office and apartment building.

Except for four houses of three story construction, the typical house (about 65%) in the village is of two stories, although the upper floor may be used only as a storage area.

Pre-1955 houses mostly are made of adobe bricks and plastered over with stucco. Clay is available near the Rio Grande and the adobes were made by the owner and at a relatively low cost in money. Newer houses are made of ceramic brick building tile which is manufactured locally. Fausto operates the major brick yard in the village and there are two smaller operations on the fringes of the village. Bricks sell for about 80 *centimos* apiece. Although adobe construction is still permissible, nobody today uses anything but brick for homes.

Both old and new houses use the traditional curved roofing tiles typical of Mediterranean area architecture; these too are made locally. A newly introduced mineral-fiber compound sold in sheets, and corrugated to facilitate water runoff, is used to roof chicken houses, storage sheds, and the like, but has not been extensively adopted for houses.

The interiors of the houses vary, but each has a kitchen, a formal parlor, and two or three bedrooms. The modal number of rooms per house is four, although this figure may be misleading since often one room will have two alcoves which serve as bedrooms, but do not qualify as separate rooms. This is a feature of the older houses; new houses usually are not built with these alcoves.

The bathroom is often an addition to the older house and is "tacked on" to the house on the corral side.

Central heating is rare in the village. Some houses have a *gloria*: a fire pit outside the house with ducts leading under the floor. The upstairs portion of the house is invariably cold in the winter. The kitchen stove is the main source of heat, although some residents use portable butane space heaters which can be moved about from room to room. This can be expensive, since the gas bottle which gives 70 hours of heat cost 122 pesetas and a normal heater costs about

3,000 pesetas. Most people make do with a brazier under a table fitted with "skirts". Soft coal is burned and throws off a fair amount of heat and one may warm his toes by placing his feet on the wooden frame that holds the metal pan. Bedrooms almost always are unheated and many people, even the hardiest, will pre-heat the bed, using a hot water bottle or a heated brick wrapped in a cloth. In the summers thick walls and continually drawn blinds keep out the heat and, even in mid-afternoon, most houses are not uncomfortably hot.

It is impossible to generalize about the average household furniture and decoration beyond the obvious statement that income and tastes vary and these are the determining factors. Rugs are infrequent except in the homes of the well-to-do, and not always there. Wall decorations are few and include polychrome religious pictures and pictures of family members. Most bedrooms have a crucifix over the bed and, in some cases, a plaster statue of Christ or the Virgin Mary on a shelf or table. Books and magazines are usually found displayed in the homes of professionals, such as the *practicante* or the schoolteachers. While the parlor is the most elegant room in the house, it is little used except on "formal" occasions; most of the social life in the house takes place in the kitchen, which is a simple room.

For a village of its size, El Pinar has a large number of business establishments, surprisingly because the village is not an area trade center. Most numerous are the bars, thirteen in all. In addition to serving wine and liquors, the bars serve coffee and soft drinks; some offer light meals to travelers, and all act as a sort of community center where people can gather to play cards and watch television.

There are several grocery stores, including one that is a member of the "SPAR" chain, three butcher shops, four bread bakeries and a confectioners, four cloth and home supply shops, two hardware stores, a barbershop, a shoe repair shop, and a number of feed and grain suppliers. Most of these enterprises are operated from small stores on the ground floor of a house with the family living quarters upstairs. Some of the shops have show windows and signs; many do not. Most of the stores are located on the plaza or nearby on adjacent streets.

Few of the shopkeepers are able to earn a living strictly from their stores and it is quite common to find the husband working at a trade while his wife runs the store. Since few shopkeepers or artisans earn enough to support a family, many have multiple occupations or business interests in the village. In many cases wives and children will tend the shop while the husband is working in a refinery or in the

Typical village street. The tobacco shop and a bakery is located in the building with signs (left center of photo). The house on its right, while inhabited, still lacks the stucco coating over the brick exterior.

fields. For example, several bars are owned by *resineros* who leave the bar operation to members of their family. One butcher runs a furniture store in the same building and also uses his DKW van as a taxi.

Pedro's bar serves as the bus station, the depot for freight trucking lines, and as an outlet for the sale of milk and fresh vegetables which he produces at his farm. While he is at the farm, the business is run by his wife and children. One of the bakers served as a municipal official in another village until his transfer in 1967; another runs the village tobacco shop in the same building as the bakery.

A blacksmith takes care of shoeing mules and the repair of farm carts as well as general metal work and Paco, the plumber, also runs a small general repair shop and a taxi. Most village men prefer to fix their own machines but all occasionally use the services of these shops.

One family opened a sweater-making business; they purchased a loom and turned out made-to-measure sweaters and other garments. This business has attracted a number of customers from the other *pueblos* in the area. A regular tailor in the village makes men's suits. On a less formal basis, a number of women take in sewing or will make dresses and one woman operates as a hairdresser.

Two motion picture theaters operate on Sunday evenings and fiestas. Movies are very popular in the rural areas of Spain, but the cinemas in El Pinar tend to show very old movies, usually imports from Mexico and Argentina, in contrast to the cinema in Villa Roman which has shown first run films of both domestic and foreign production.

Banking services are provided through the *Caja de Ahorros y Monte de Piedad* (a savings and loan association) and a branch of a national bank, both of these facilities being located in Leyes. The Leyes branch bank maintains a sub-office in the village and the clerk handles some business during the evenings for people who were unable to get to Leyes. Any normal transaction, including the exchange of foreign currency, can be handled by Francisco, the bank clerk, whose regular occupation is as a clerk in the City Hall.

In addition to fixed stores and shops, peddlers daily sell their wares on the Plaza. Some come by truck, but most are people from neighboring villages who arrive in burro or mule drawn carts selling vegetables, clothing, and a bewildering array of goods. Many of the El Pinar merchants also travel to other villages to sell their wares. Next to fruit and vegetables, the most frequently seen goods are clothing and kitchen utensils, plates, and pottery. The peddler's arrivals are heralded by the town crier who is hired by them to go through the streets tooting his whistle to get attention and then shouting out the wares for sale. When there is an official announcement to be made, the crier announces the news with two toots of the whistle instead of the customary one.

Apart from the resin industries and the agricultural operations, the only other major business operations are the brickyards. Fausto's brickyard employs several younger men and is by far the largest. Annually he turns out almost enough bricks to build fifteen houses. The other brickyards are much smaller and operate sporadically, using household members as unpaid labor.

Services are provided through the City Hall and through the national government. Water and street cleaning are village responsibilities; in addition, the City Hall provides the usual administrative support and record keeping. The major services are, however, provided directly by the national government. The five man *Guardia Civil* detachment is maintained by the State as are the ten schoolteachers and the entire school program. The Municipal Secretary, while serving the village, is a member of a national administrative corps and receives his salary from the State.

El Pinar has a resident veterinarian, physician, and *practicante* to minister to health needs. These are State appointed but receive some small salary from the village while earning their income by the charging of fees.

While not an official in the normal sense of the word, the village priest is, in this officially Roman Catholic country, in effect a State employee and receives a subsidy for his maintenance. He resides in El Pinar and is aided by a young coadjutor who divides his services between Leyes and El Pinar.

The two most important villages in the *comarca* are Leyes and Villa Roman. The former is a village of approximately 2,300 people located to the south of El Pinar; the latter has about the same population and is located to the west. Leyes is the wealthiest of the villages; it is on the railroad and serves as the break point for rail freight shipments. In Leyes are the main banks and the storage facilities of the *Servicio Nacional de Cereales*, the government grain purchasing agency. The El Pinar farmers take their grain to the SNC agency for sale after the harvest. In addition there has been much intermarriage between the villages and kinship ties are strong. Leyes offers a dance hall superior to the one in El Pinar and its *fiesta* always attracts the villagers of El Pinar. The bars in Leyes are better equipped and more attractive and it gives the impression of being a socially more active village.

Villa Roman is the headquarters of the *Communidad* that includes both El Pinar and Leyes, as well as six other villages that share ownership in the pines. The village authorities by their astute and aggressive actions have made the village an educational center. There is an *Instituto Laboral* (a technical trade school) in the village and a school for forestry *capataces,* the *capataz* being a skilled forest technician but not university educated. *The Servicio de Extensión Agrária* (Agricultural Extension Service) has an office in Villa Roman serving the *comarca.* Official relations between Villa Roman and El Pinar have been strained for over seventy-five years due to disputes over profits from communally owned pines, but this strain has not been seriously evident of late. There is no hostility evident between the peoples; simply, most villages will pass through Leyes en route to Segovia or on business and will stop for a drink there. To go to Villa Roman means taking the dirt road from El Pinar and, since little business is done in Villa Roman, and since it is not on a major travel route from El Pinar, one doesn't go there except specifically on business or to visit family members.

Resin refineries in Villa Roman and in Leyes are smaller and produce less than the refineries in El Pinar. Nevertheless, Leyes is the economic leader in the *comarca* and Villa Roman has assumed political leadership in dealing with the provincial government.

The other villages are smaller and less economically diversified. San Blas has approximately 1,500 inhabitants and is primarily agricultural, although it owns some pine trees. Its major fame comes, according to the young men in El Pinar, from the supposed fact that the village has the prettiest girls in the *comarca.*

Ramos, El Hoyo, San Miguel and a cluster of small villages near this latter village all lie south and east of El Pinar. These are small farm villages with populations of less than 500 and connected to El Pinar by dirt roads. Ties here are less intense than to Leyes, but again there has been inter-village marriage and some migration to El Pinar by people from these villages prior to 1950.

While some villages are wealthier due to income from the pines and populations vary, all of these villages can be said to form a homogeneous socio-cultural whole. Insofar as customs and patterns of social relations are concerned, one is essentially similar to all the others.

Demographic Characteristics

The national census of 1960 and municipal records, especially the *Padron Municipal*, which is the municipal civil register, showed that the population of El Pinar as of 1 January 1967 was 2,320 people. Of these 1,161 were males and 1,159 were females.

While this figure represents the officially registered population, the actual resident population is somewhat lower. Many residents leave the village to work in France on a contract basis and are absent from six to eight months of the year. A number of others are students or workers in large cities and come to the village only during vacation periods. Approximately 200 men and women were known to be working abroad in 1969.

Though officially registered as residents of the village, members of the *Guardia Civil* detachment, schoolteachers, and some municipal functionaries are, in effect, temporary residents. *Guardia Civil* staff are transferred periodically and schoolteachers may come and go every year. In many of the less "desirable" villages, a new schoolteacher every year is normal; however, El Pinar is considered as a good village and teachers tend to stay on permanently.

The steady growth of population of El Pinar from 1900 to 1950 led the planning authorities in Segovia to project a steady increase through the year 2000. However, changes in economic conditions and a continued exodus from rural areas to the cities were not foreseen at the time the projection was made. El Pinar is slowly losing population as are other villages of the *comarca* and villages throughout rural Spain. Between 1941 and 1964, the Province lost 10,138 people to outmigration, while 125 men and 141 women left El Pinar permanently during the decade 1950-1960. In 1966 six families—some 25 people—left town for work in Madrid and Bilbao. The great majority of these emigrants are people between the ages of 18 and 35, in effect, the youth of the village.

With emigration and long-term absentees and the essentially transitory residents, the average daily resident population of El Pinar is about 1,850 people.

The population of El Pinar is homogeneous; only 470 inhabitants were born out of the village and most of these were born elsewhere in the Province. The population is entirely Caucasian and Roman Catholic. One gypsy family lives in the village but is so well integrated into the life of the village that it is not considered "different" by the people. A few African students, who attend the *Instituto Laboral* located in a nearby village, come to El Pinar from time to time to

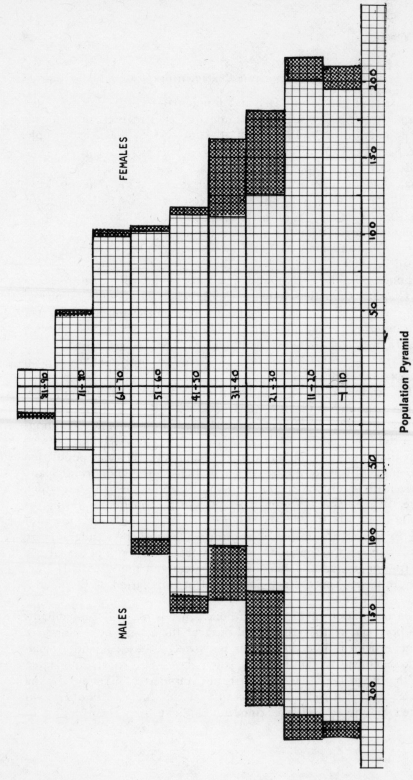

Population Pyramid

dances or to *fiestas*. They are received with absolutely no sign of discrimination: indeed, there are no ethnic or religiously based social problems in the *comarca*.

Marriages are usually with partners from the village, although probably about 40% of all marriages are contracted with partners from one of the nearby villages and almost invariably with another Castillian. Marriages to non-Castillians are infrequent but not unknown; during my stay one girl became engaged to a boy from Barcelona. Despite the large numbers of men and women who have gone to France, few marriages with foreigners have taken place. One man living in the village had a French wife, and the last "international" marriage was between a Spanish man and a German girl who took up residence in his native village of Villa Roman.

The Provincial birthrate in 1960 was 20.4 per 1,000 and the mortality rate was 8.54 per 1,000. These figures approximate the national average for that period.

There appears to be a decrease in the number of children per family in the last ten or fifteen years, although exact statistics are not available for the *pueblo*. Birth control is known and apparently widely practiced by villagers, although most people are understandably reluctant to discuss it. The Church approved rhythm method is well known and seems to be slowly replacing the traditional *coitus interruptus* method common in peasant areas. Contraceptive pills, known in Spanish as the *"anti-bebe"* pill or simply *"La Pildora"*, are available by prescription but their use is rare in the rural areas as is the use of contraceptives in general. They are not stocked in the village pharmacy and are difficult to obtain even in larger cities.

The average household size is 4 people. Census data lists 94 one-person households but further examination of each case showed that most of these people, widows, widowers, and elderly couples, lived in the same house as members of their family and socially belonged to that household.

Migration to the village has been practically negligible in the last 20 years. Data from an unpublished survey by *Caritas Española*, the Spanish Catholic Charity organization, show that there were no immigrants to El Pinar during the 1950-1960 decade. Only one family of four came to the village after 1960; this was a family from a neighboring village who came to work in one of the sawmills. The general migration pattern in the Provinces is to move from village to city with little inter-village mobility.

The Province has consistently maintained one of the lowest il-

literacy rates in Spain. In 1910 the rate of 39.40% illiterates made the
Province the sixth most literate in the nation. In 1960 only 3% were
illiterate and the Province ranked 11th in literacy with only very small
differences separating it from higher ranking provinces. In El Pinar
there were 72 illiterates in the population over the age of ten. Fifty-
five of these were women and 17 were men and all of these were
over 60 years of age. The remaining 11 persons were physically or
mentally handicapped. Part of the explanation for this phenomenon
is that the region of the Old Castile traditionally has had a high
literacy rate and, furthermore, government efforts in adult education
have been quite successful in teaching older people to read and write.

Political Organization

El Pinar has a Mayor-Council government as do all Spanish municipalities. The Mayor is appointed by the Civil Governor of the Province and serves an indefinite term of office. The City Councilmen
serve three-year-terms and may be re-elected or re-appointed as the
case may be. One third of the council is elected by the *Vecinos
Cabezas de Familias*, the married men who head a household, and
some widows and other adult persons who qualify as household heads.
Another third of the Council is elected by the workers through their
trade union organization, the *Sindicato*. The remaining third are
chosen by members of the "civic and professional entities". In El
Pinar, this latter group is appointed by the Mayor after consultation
with the remaining member of the Council. The Mayor and Council
are all local residents although the Provincial Governor could appoint
a non-resident to the Mayor's post. For many years the Mayor and
Council were subservient to the village's *cacique*, but with the passing
of Eusibio Moreno's power around 1960, they were more or less freed
of such "bossism". The Mayor of El Pinar is a farmer; the councilmen also are farmers and workers at the resin refineries. Local businessmen do not dominate the Council nor does any group control or
even try to control it.

The effectiveness of local government varies from village to village.
In contrast to those of El Pinar, the village authorities of Villa Roman
are a very active and politically sophisticated group. In general, village
governments have little real power and even less money with which
to operate, and major decisions are made for them at the Provincial
or national level, as in the case of the resin crisis. (*cf.* pp. 99 ff).

Civil action groups are unknown in El Pinar. The Mayor is a local

man well known to all, as are the Councilmen and other functionaries. Any citizen may speak out at the monthly Council meetings
(although few do so) and the informal communications system of a
small town insures that the leaders know what the people are thinking at all times. Consensus or division of opinion on any problem
is immediately recognized in the village without any apparent need
for specialized groups to take charge of mustering consent or opposition.

It is the government—national, provincial, and local—that bears the
burden of seeking solutions to problems. These holding offices are auto-
matically in position of power by virtue of that office. However,
villagers repeatedly pointed out that those with wealth are usually in
a position to influence community life and some governmental decisions.

When asked to name the *two* most influential citizens in El Pinar,
both the village leaders and the general population were in agreement. Most frequently named were Eusibio Moreno and the village
priest. Not all of the people were happy at the influence of these two
men, but none denied the reality of that influence.

When asked to name *six* additional influential people, most informants had a very difficult time in replying. Most indicated the civil
authorities in general, especially the Commandant of the *Guardia
Civil* post. In all cases, it was the office and not the man that was
cited; influence and power are functions of the position in El Pinar.
Virtually none of the villagers distinguish between power and influence. They see the two phenomena as being aspects of the same
phenomenon not separable in reality.

A lack of cooperation between people is directly related to patterns
of influence. Each villager, regardless of wealth or occupation, feels
that he is the moral equal of any man. Each person prefers to go
his own way in his business. This individualism, well recognized by
informants, leads to a situation where no group of private citizens can
be too influential because practically nobody will pay any attention
to them. Having rejected the domination by *caciques* of the past, and
granted the independent spirit of the people and their failure to
achieve cooperative groups, influence and power is effectively left in
the hands of the officials. The villagers—peasants and professionals
alike—are agreed that they are "a hard people to govern". They see
the need for a government strong enough to force them into unity.
They say that the average Spaniard is like a mule; he will not move
unless threatened with a stick.

An old story, which antedates both the ill-fated Second Republic and the present Regime, illustrates their attitude toward government. —It seems God came upon a poor shepherd who was known to have lived a good life. God wished to show his generosity to this young Spanish lad and thus granted him three wishes. "I wish", said the boy, "for a beautiful country," "Done", said God. "Then, I wish for a strong and handsome people to inhabit it," said the boy. "Done", said God. Then the lad thought for a while and said. "Lord, give our country and our people a good government." God looked down in pity at the lad and replied, "My son, even I cannot do that."

The public concept of the ideal leader can be summarized by noting that the Spaniards here prefer a strong and forceful person who takes charge of an operation and gives the orders in such a way they are carried out quickly and efficiently. The leader who cannot give orders and enforce them is not a leader by village standards.

This concept does not mean that the villagers prefer a dictator in their midst; the "ideal leader" must first have certain qualities which engender the respect of the people. Lacking these qualities, even the most strong-willed of would-be leaders would run into an insurmountable wall of public opposition.

Figure 4 shows the most important characteristics of a leader as seen by the leadership group. In general, the population as a whole shares the same opinions about these ideal qualities.

The three major qualities the people look for in a leader are: 1st, good moral character; 2nd, a "decent" educational background; and 3rd, the competence necessary to do the job well.

Influential friends are matters of real and ideal importance. The leaders pointed out, repeatedly, that a leader must have "good contacts" to function well and that no leader could expect to get the things his town needed without some degree of political influence. Also, granted the realities of appointive office in Spain, even the potentially most desirable leader could not get a chance to lead without holding an office—and to hold office requires political influence of some kind.

High moral character is the first requisite of a leader. In El Pinar, service to the community is not necessarily a stepping stone to an office, although it is not something to be entirely overlooked. What villagers have difficulty understanding is the meaning of the term "service"; one leader noted that merely being a good citizen and neighbor is in itself a service to be appreciated by all. Lacking the organized facilities of civic clubs and similar groups, there is really no

FIGURE 4

**Relative Importance of Individual Characteristics Related to
Holding An Important Office**

Characteristic	Average Rating
Good Moral Character	3.00
Good Education	2.89
"Political Influence"	2.86
Friendliness toward people	2.67
Honorable Family name	2.44
Has influential friends in town	2.38
Has extraordinary personal abilities	2.22
Is successful businessman	2.11
Length of residence in town	2.00
Service to community	1.78
Occupation	1.67
Property or Wealth possessed	1.67

Very Important—3;   Somewhat Important—2;   Unimportant—1

way for the citizen of El Pinar to participate in civic action programs; thus, "service to community" in American terms becomes meaningless.

In El Pinar, leadership has traditionally been vested in an official (usually government appointed) position but similar power of a quasi-legal nature has been exercised by a *cacique* through economic domination of the village. No tradition of popular leadership exists in the area. With the decline of the *cacique's* power previously noted, coercive power is now vested only in the offices of Mayor, Priest, and Commandant of the *Guardia Civil* post. Only the Priest has actually attempted to exert authority openly and has earned the general dislike of the village for his efforts. The Mayor and the nine man Council have some power over local affairs but rarely ever attempt to use it. The *Guardia Civil* detachment is led by a sergeant and tends to act more as an informal peacemaker when it must act at all. The people like and respect the detachment members but are not afraid of them since, in their view, law-abiding citizens need never fear the law under ordinary circumstances.

The villagers equate leadership with coercive power. This does not mean that a dictator would be acceptable; the leader must have certain human qualities that elicit peoples' respect. The leader must be competent to do his job; job competence is more important than any specific educational title. He must also be friendly with the people, respect them, and be respected by them. The "ideal leader" is expected to have a good set of useful contacts and pull in government agencies at the provincial level. The leader who cannot manipulate the government cannot hope to succeed.

No such "ideal leader" exists in the village or in any of the other villages of the *comarca*. If he did, it is doubtful that he could succeed in the local social milieu. "This pueblo", said one knowledgeable informant, "is the enemy of cooperation"—a dictum that could be generalized to cover most of the villages of the *comarca*.

Perhaps the closest to being an ideal leader from the villagers' point of view is Don Jaime, the 46-year-old *practicante* who was elected to the City Council by a record majority vote over three opponents and who became Lieutenant Mayor in 1968. A native of the Province of Leon, Don Jaime fought as a young boy in the Civil War and later served as a medical corpsman in the Spanish "Blue Division" which fought with the Germans on the Russian front during World War II. He first came to El Pinar in 1957 with his wife, a native of Madrid.

In addition to his medical practice, Don Jaime soon interested himself in the youth of the village and became active in the *Frente de Juventudes*, a government sponsored youth program which later became known as the *Organización Juvenil Española*. A likeable and gregarious person, Don Jaime gives the appearance of perpetual motion as he darts about the village in his Citroen 2 CV car dispensing medicine, giving innoculations, delivering babies, telling jokes, buying drinks, and attending to municipal business. He has achieved a level of popularity never reached by any of the other municipal authorities.

Ambrosio Aguilar, the Mayor, is a native of the village and a farmer by occupation. Ambrosio, while friendly, is a less extroverted person and the necessity of tending his fields leaves him little time to circulate around the village as does Don Jaime. Appointed Mayor in 1965, Ambrosio also serves as *Jefe Local del Movimiento, i.e.,* local head of the Movement which is the national organization that co-opted the Falangist Party and is the major political organization in Spain. In practice, the Mayor and *Jefe Local* positions are always held by the same person in Spain. Beyond a few ceremonies, and seeing that the City Hall is draped with flags on holidays, Ambrosio has little to do with the *Movimiento's* affairs and policies which are set at a much higher government level. No one, including himself, is quite sure why Ambrosio was named Mayor since he had never been a prominent personage in the village. However, he is an honorable man and loyal—but not fanatically—to Franco.

The life of a Mayor or Councilman in villages like El Pinar is one characterized by routine decisions and administrative work broken once in a while by some crisis which most municipal authorities are ill prepared to cope with. Since neither Mayor nor Councilmen receive a salary for the job, all have to be employed in some other occupation and serve the village on a part-time basis. Only large cities, such as Madrid or Barcelona, have fulltime salaried Mayors.

One crisis that faced El Pinar was the threatened *resinero* strike which is discussed in Chapter 5. Another was the poisoning of the village water supply in the summer of 1969.

In early July of 1969, a farmer found the partially decomposed bodies of some pigs in the river near Hoyo Paloma, about two kilometers upstream from the village water supply pumphouse. Later during that week, other dead pigs were found in brush near the shore of the Rio Grande. A search by Forest Guards and *Guardia Civil* discovered yet more carcasses. At about this time many villagers became ill with intestinal disorders and an analysis of the water showed that it had become contaminated and thus unfit for drinking. Also, the pipes carrying water to the houses were contaminated and the City Hall announced that all drinking water should be boiled prior to drinking. Leyes, Villa Roman, and other villages drawing potable water from the river issued warnings and the situation began to attract attention in Segovia. It soon became apparent that the pigs had been dumped into the river by farmers who did not want to report that the animals were infected with African Swine Pest, a highly contagious disease among swine.

The initial pressures on Ambrosio were mild since most villagers thought that the cutting of the piped water would last only a few days. However, when the extent of the pollution and the fact that over 100 dead pigs had been found came to public attention, the cries of outrage became stronger. As the wheat harvest was in process, Ambrosio had secured a two month leave of absence from the Civil Governor and turned the duties of his office over to Don Jaime. The pressures on the Lieutenant Mayor soon became almost unbearable as the national press printed news of the contaminated waters and the villagers began to face the possibility of having no running water during the hottest months of the year. To get drinking water, the villagers used a spring on the outskirts of the village or brought water from wells on the Rio Chico farm plots where the water was pure. For about two weeks water was brought in through the existing pipes from the old water source north of town, but pressure was low and water flowed only a few hours in the mornings and evenings. To make things worse, the pump broke down completely and had to be repaired.

Don Jaime's life became extremely difficult. People stopped him on the streets to complain about the water situation, his telephone rang constantly, each call bringing a new complaint. It was necessary for him to make several trips a week to Segovia to see about getting the pump repaired. At one point he even thought of asking the Army to bring tank trailers of water to supply the village's needs. To add to the burden, he had to meet an increased demand for his medical services when people became ill with gastrointestinal disturbances or related illnesses. A possible case of typhoid was discovered. In addition, the two pump operators balked at having to work at the old pump since it was far from the village; later, the same men refused to work a different schedule when the regular pump was restored to operation. Local politics made it impossible for them to be fired.

In the meanwhile, the investigation seeking the farmers who had thrown the pigs in the river started off slowly. The indications were that they were from Ramos but no one in that village would admit to the act nor were the *Guardia Civil* able to determine who was responsible. This struck the villagers of El Pinar as rather odd— the presence of swine pest in a village becomes immediately known to all and the death of even one pig is a matter of general knowledge even in villages as large as El Pinar. When Don Jaime's complaints finally reached the Civil Governor's ear, that authority called a meeting of all Mayors, and veterinarians in the affected area and insisted they find the guilty parties. Apparently pressure was also put on the Provincial commander of the *Guardia Civil* who stimulated the efforts of lower echelon officers. The culprits, two brothers and the veterinarian of Ramos, were soon discovered and later given a stiff fine.

During the entire crisis, Ambrosio seldom could be found in the village and took little action to remedy the situation; after all, he was on leave of absence. Few of the Councilmen took an active part in solving the problem of supplying water to the village; some became involved only to protect the pump operators when they refused to work. No one thought this was correct behavior, but then no one expected very much of the Councilmen in the first place.

At the end of the crisis, with fresh water running through uncontaminated pipes, Don Jaime was able to relax. But he was a profoundly unhappy man and talked constantly of quitting his position. He despaired of ever getting any positive action out of Ambrosio or the

Council. His wife, Doña Mari-Bel, also urged him to stop wasting his time on "ingrates" and "bums"—two of the milder terms she applied to the village authorities. Instead of gratitude for his service, Don Jaime received only abuse from the public. Since the villagers saw that he was the only person actively involved in trying to solve the water crisis, they quite naturally took their complaints to him and, when he could not satisfy their demands immediately, they perceived him as having caused their troubles.

There are few rewards for political service in the village beyond being able to "take care" of some relative or friend. Without sufficient funds or facilities, village authorities tend to do only as much as they must to maintain their jobs and even in times of crisis most would rather not "get involved", an attitude that will be discussed further in Chapter 7.

Typical two wheeled farm cart returning home from the fields. Automobile tires have largely replaced the traditional ironshod wooden wheel on carts. In the background is El Pinar's clock tower.

CHAPTER III

Social and Economic Life

Social Stratification

WITHIN THE PROVINCE there are three broad social classes. A small upper class group is comprised of a few old families with titles of nobility, some of the very wealthy industrialists, high government leaders, and church leaders such as the Bishop. A middle class is made up of lower ranking military officers, government officials, clergy, small industrialists, businessmen, and professionals. These groups live mostly in the capital city and are almost exclusively urban in life style and world view. The most numerous group, about 75% of the Province's population, is a working class composed of farmers and employed workers. At the very bottom of the social scale are gypsies and some itinerant day laborers. This group is the least stable, the members moving about the country frequently; most are from other regions of Spain and are not Castillians.

In El Pinar differentiations based upon income and occupation are minimal, for the most part. At the top are the two wealthiest families who own the major resin refineries. Both families worked their way up to great wealth from almost literally nothing.

The life of Eusibio Moreno reads something like an American Horatio Alger story. With minimal schooling, he had to work for a living at an early age in the forests, somehow accumulating enough money to build a small resin refinery and sawmill. Though his plant burned down several times, he was always able to rebuild and improve his operations, especially with use of the insurance money received from the fires. Though the villagers had a number of doubts as to the origin of these fires, by the Civil War Eusibio had become one of the wealthiest men of the area. After a short period in jail—he was put there by the Falangist groups supporting Franco—Eusibio emerged again on good terms with the new government and became the dominant person in El Pinar. According to local legend, while fleeing from the village during the war, he loaded a truck with barrels normally used for resin. The truck hit a bump and a barrel fell off, broke open, and showered the road with coins. Eusibio had his driver keep on without stopping to recover the money.

While he was never Mayor, the incumbent always had to defer to Eusibio's wishes, as did the Council. He and his family built a large three-story mansion across from the main factory, next to the *Guardia Civil* headquarters. Slowly, and for reasons never clearly established, Eusibio's power began to wane around 1960, and he was no longer the undisputed *cacique* of El Pinar as he had been for so many years.

The Moreno's still live in the village and Eusibio worked every day in his refinery office until his death at the age of 87 in 1967. The family property is scattered all over Spain, Eusibio being a shareholder in foreign as well as domestic industries. All his children were educated at private schools out of the village; several of the sons and grandsons are university graduates.

The family of Eusibio Moreno has stayed aloof from village activities and rarely socializes with the rest of the village. The family has few friends and is disliked by most of the village. Eusibio was blamed for holding back the village's development during his *cacique* period; the most common complaint being that he "never did anything for the village." The old man attended early Mass every Sunday, thus avoiding contact with most of the village; on other days, he stayed in his house or office. The children are more sociable; some of the sons stop for a drink on the Plaza after Mass or during fiestas, but normally the Moreno family has kept to itself behind the walls and fences of its mansion.

The other leading family, that of Juan San Miguel, also has a resin refinery in El Pinar as well as large landholdings in other provinces, other factories and refineries, and varied business dealings. The San Miguels' spend much of the year living away from the village, but there is usually at least one son in residence to watch over the family businesses. This family is much more highly regarded than the Morenos, generally being more sociable and less aloof. Also, Juan has helped several men get started in business by lending them money and providing other assistance through his influence in the government.

The Province of Segovia, along with most of Old Castile, falls into a category described by Spanish social scientists as "*clases medias*"—a largely non-industrial middle class grouping of people in the cities with a larger core group of landowning or permanent leaseholding peasantry scattered in country villages.[1]

There is a visible distinction between the rich and the poor in Spain, but the term social stratification is too strong to describe social differentiation in El Pinar. There is some self-imposed and village sanctioned segregation between groups or categories of people. In many cases this is regarded as necessary and as a part of the obligations of one's job. For example, the *Guardia Civil* must hold themselves somewhat aloof from the people if they are to be objective in carrying out their duties as police officers. The village priest should not become too closely allied with any one group since he is responsible for the spiritual wellbeing of all. Unhappily, the priest in El Pinar never lived up to this, and allied himself with the Morenos. However, since the alliance between clergy and the rich and powerful in Spain has a long tradition, the peoples' criticisms of Don Eugenio were tempered by the fact that they really didn't expect that he would have acted otherwise.

With the egalitarian ethic in the village, snobbishness is frowned upon and often openly ridiculed. As everybody in the village knows everybody else, the attempt by any person or family to put on airs or assume poses thought to be inappropriate is immediately noticed and criticized.

Excepting the Morenos and the San Miguels, who are so rich as to be almost outside the village social system, the top people in the social order are those with the title of *Don*. For the most part these are the professionals and major functionaries such as the physician, priest, Municipal Secretary, veterinarian, schoolteachers, and pharmacist. The normal mode of employing the title is to place *Don* (*Doña* for women) before his first name; for example while the priest's full name is Eugenio Martin Gil, he is always addressed as Don Eugenio when speaking with him.

Every adult Spaniard is entitled to be called *Don* or *Doña* regardless of social position. Letters are so addressed and official documents carry the designation. However, in oral usage, only those who hold specific positions are actually addressed by the honorific title. Thus, old Pablo Alvarez, a retired *resinero* with little schooling or income, receives mail addressed to Don Pablo Alvarez but no one calls him Don Pablo nor does he expect to be called that. In the El Pinar area,

[1] *cf.* Linz and DeMiguel's analysis of "the Eight Spains," (1966).

it is the profession or occupation that determines the oral usage of *Don* in referring to or speaking to a person. The true test of a person's claim to the honorific title is passed when he is spoken of as Don so-and-so when he is not present. Thus, in referring to the priest, he is always Don Eugenio whether or not he is present when his name is spoken.

The Andalusian useage of *Señorito* (*cf.* Pitt-Rivers, 1954) as an honorific title is little used in Old Castille. When a villager is deemed worthy of special respect because of his age, wealth, or power, he may be addressed as *Señor* followed by his first name in a manner similar to the use of *Don*. Thus old Pablo Alvarez is often addressed as Señor Pablo by those younger than he as a sign of their respect.

For the most part, villagers call each other by their first names. While almost everyone has a nickname, it is considered impolite to address a person by it, although he is often referred to by the nickname in his absence.

For all the egalitarian sentiments, social differences are noticeable in the daily round of village life. Usually the *Dons* are expected to wear a coat and tie in public and to act in a dignified manner. They must be pleasant with the ordinary folk, but not condescending. Unless their occupations such as Agricultural Extension agents require it, they must not mingle too freely with the working class people. Yet they must never show reluctance to shake hands or to drink with the people. Generally their socializing is spent in the company of their peers, usually at one of the village bars or in their homes.

Marriages are almost always between social equals, but there are exceptions. At the working class level, sons of farmers marry daughters of *resineros,* shopkeepers daughters marry farmers' sons, and so on. The main consideration is that the mate's family be honorable. It is not that the people are unaware of socio-economic differences; rather that these differences tend to be minimal. Also, villagers judge a man less on his monetary worth than on his personal characteristics. An honorable man may hold any occupation, and while one job may be considered as being better than another, this comparison does not carry over to the person holding the job. There are dishonorable men whose position entitles them to be called *Don*.

With the general opening up of opportunity for peasants in Spain and the increased chances of a peasant's son becoming a schoolteacher —and thus a *Don*—the whole system of honorific titles seems to be declining in importance.

Daily Celebrations

Life in the village has, despite seasonal variations, a certain sameness to it that is comforting to the older generation and annoying to the younger. For most farmers, the day begins at sunrise. As his wife prepares the breakfast coffee and bread, the farmer goes to the corral adjoining his house to feed his team of mules, his cow, and his swine. After breakfast, he usually hitches up the mules and goes to his fields to work. His wife tries to go back to bed for a few hours more sleep if possible, but she is usually in the Plaza doing the day's shopping with the other women by ten o'clock.

Most villagers do not like to get up early, especially in the cold winter months. Even in the cities where most of the houses have central heating and where life is more comfortable, few people are to be seen on the streets before 9 A.M. However, the farmers and *resineros* have no choice and must be out in the early morning.

The daily life of El Pinar can be marked by the church bells which announce the two morning Masses, the evening Rosary, and—in special cases—emergencies. The bell in the clock tower also strikes the hours but few pay it much heed.

About 10 A.M. most stores are open and the Plaza is swarming with women buying food from itinerant peddlars or from established shops. The resin refineries are in operation, the City Hall staff is at work, and the school starts its daily classes. The Postal Agent and his daughter have begun to sort out the mail and will deliver it around the village before noon. A small knot of people gather at the clinic for medical treatment and soon after they are treated the car of Don Jaime, the *practicante,* can be seen darting through the streets as he makes his rounds of patients to give injections or treatment.

By 11 A.M., the streets are relatively quiet; people are at work in the refineries, in their homes, at school, in their businesses, or in the fields or pines.

At about 2 P.M. most people eat lunch, normally the largest meal of the day. The farmers who are working outlying fields usually take their lunches with them—bread and sausage and some wine—or have the lunch brought them by some child of theirs on a bicycle or motorcycle. The *siesta,* while a disappearing custom, nevertheless is still observed, especially in the summer when the afternoon heat becomes almost unbearable. Shops and refineries close from about one or two to about four or five in the afternoon for lunch and *siesta.* The streets are again deserted except for someone scurrying off on an errand.

It is in the evening that El Pinar comes alive. After five in the afternoon the bars fill up with the *jubilados,* the old men who are retired.
This is the time to sit in the bar and drink a glass of wine and play
tute or *mus*—the two favorite card games. By seven the crowds have
grown and the bars on the Plaza are filled with men laughing, talking,
playing cards, and generally enjoying themselves. The *Guardia Civil*
will be in the bars as well, not in any police capacity but to talk, drink
coffee, and wait for the evening busses to arrive from Segovia and Valladolid. The scene is liveliest in the warm months; in the winter few
sally forth from their houses and the bars are less crowded.

The evening Rosary is said at seven in the summer and some women
—for men virtually never attend—go to the church for the evening de-
votions. Many are recent widows or girls whose father or other close
relatives have died; a few are the *beatas,* a rather sarcastic term applied by Spaniards to the women who "live in Church." After the de-
votions, Don Eugenio will head for the bars and have his evening coffee and chat with the men.

By eight o'clock the two busses have arrived and the people met by
their families, the bus drivers stop for a drink, the evening mail is
sorted and the Post Office opened for mail pickup, and people going
on to other villages along the bus line get off for a few minutes break
in their journey. Since the two busses, the one from Valladolid and the
other from Segovia, meet at El Pinar, the village is a transfer point and
one bus cannot leave until the other has arrived. Thus there is always
a crowd of transients in the bar to add to the noise and general happy
confusion.

Few of the people in the Plaza at night are farmers; most are too
tired to come and have to get up early the next day and thus eat supper and retire by 10 P.M. Few women are to be seen in the Plaza; most
of them have chores at home to attend to. Many are young men who,
having nothing else to do, go from bar to bar singing, playing cards
and passing the time.

In the summer people like to come out of their homes and sit in the
evening cool in front of their houses. Small clusters may be seen as
neighbors pull up chairs to chat, the women often sewing as they talk.
People passing by say hello or, if not on speaking terms with the
group, say nothing and look the other way. A walk from the Plaza to
the clock tower which, at three in the afternoon takes five minutes, is
apt to take half an hour in the evening as people stop to chat with
those sitting in front of the houses.

Supper is usually eaten at 10 P.M. and tends to be a light meal, such as an omelet and some sausage. Since most people have an afternoon snack around five, they are not usually hungry in the evening and many eat only a very light supper immediately before going to bed. There is a tendency now for more people to eat supper at eight in the evening. There is no particular status connotation in this; generally, people eat supper whenever they feel like it without regard to what the others are doing.

Refinery workers and those who also have to be at work the next day desert the streets by about 11 P.M. By midnight of most working days everybody but the inevitable hard-core of youngsters is at home preparing for bed. The *serenos,* two of them, patrol the streets crying out the hour and the state of the weather, and by two in the morning in summer—much earlier in the winter—the town is asleep, resting to repeat the routine again the following day.

It is on Sundays that the village is most lively, for this is a day of rest and only the more necessary chores are done by the farmers. Prior to the main Mass at eleven o'clock the men and women, usually in separate groups, congregate in the Plaza in front of the Church to talk and joke, many stopping in one of the bars for a cup of coffee.

The men, and some few women, sit or stand in pews ranged across the back of the church and along the sides of the nave. The women fill up the center section of the church, alternately sitting or kneeling on canebacked chairs designed especially for this purpose. There is a constant murmur as the women and a few men participate in the recital of the litanies. Children cry; there is some whispering among the young boys, and the whole Mass is punctuated by a mild buzzing sound.

After Mass people gather again in front of the church and smoke a cigarette with their friends, gossip and pass the time. The married women usually head home to begin preparing lunch while the men and a few groups of women head for the bars for the Sunday *chateo*— the delightful custom of having an aperatif and snacks, such as fried seafoods, clams or crayfish. Bars are crowded, people are in a good mood, and they enjoy conversations with friends.

In the evening the townspeople walk down the road toward the Rio Grande for the *paseo.* Married couples walk with their children or with other couples. Formally engaged couples may walk hand in hand, and the rest of the youth of the village walk in groups segregated by sex. Groups of young men will eye groups of young women (and vice-versa) as they pass along the road, light banter is exchanged, and everyone does their best to make sure they present a good appearance.

Bars are also crowded during the late afternoon and well into the night. This is the "girls' night out" and women will cluster in the bars to watch television or gossip with their friends and relatives while the men play cards and dominoes separately. Segregation by sex is not due to any strict norm but rather seems to be a loosely accepted custom. Among the young professionals, such as schoolteachers, men and women sit together regardless of marital status and this behavior is not uncommon among the non-professionals as well. The crowds are augmented somewhat by those attending the late afternoon Mass. Many attend the Mass at 5:00 P.M. instead of the morning Mass since they need not get up early to do so. Farmers who have to do chores on Sunday will usually also attend the later Mass.

On summer Sunday evenings there is usually a dance which is attended mostly by the youth of the village. The band comes from one of the neighboring villages and invariably the music is some sort of rock and roll punctuated occasionally by slower dances. Except for a *jota* every once in a while and at the end of the dance, no traditional folk dancing is seen. Indeed, except for an occasional *jota,* there is practically no folk music or dance to be heard in the area on normal occasions. It makes little difference what the band may be playing since couples dance as they please. A married couple may be doing a slow foxtrot to the latest rock tune or two girls may be dancing the twist (or the local version thereof) to the strains of a *pasadoble.* It is at the dance that one sees the vaunted individualism of the Castillian at its most flagrant heights.

The dance is usually interrupted about ten o'clock so that the band and the dancers can eat supper, but the action resumes shortly thereafter and continues on till after midnight—the exact time depends upon how much the band is being paid or how much extra they can be paid to keep on playing. The married couples will usually drift home by midnight as will the single girls, leaving the bars and the Plaza to the men who will stay on longer. Sundays end inevitably at some late hour of the morning with the last group of young men wending their way home singing and shouting at the top of their lungs.

Bars are central to the everyday life of El Pinar. If viewed only as dispensaries of alcoholic beverages, one cannot understand the true importance of these establishments. The bar, in Spain as elsewhere, is a sort of community center where old and young, male and female may gather. Coffee is served, many bars also serve snacks, all serve Coca-Cola or some other soft drink, and all have a television set. Only relatives and the closest friends visit in each other's homes; the main social life of the town takes place, therefore, in public bars, and everyone in town patronizes them.

Enrique's is probably as typical as any bar in the *comarca*. The door opens into a small hallway whose passage is negotiated by dodging the crowd jammed in it—people always seem to be either entering or leaving Enrique's. The main room has a long wooden bar running most of its length, behind which is the usual assortment of bottles. The rest of the room is crowded with small marble topped tables (the newer bars have tables with Formica tops) and wooden straight backed chairs. There are no bar stools; to drink at the bar, you stand up.

The normal procedure is to take the first empty table and wait for the waiter to come; this is informal in village bars and if the waiter is slow, he can be encouraged by a loud clapping of hands that Spaniards use to summon waiters, *serenos* and servants. Though not done in the city in the more elegant bars, it is the custom in the *pueblos*. The drinks being ordered, people can call for a set of dominoes or a deck of cards which the bar provides without charge. The price of the first drink is, in effect, a licence to spend the whole evening in the bar without any further need for purchases.

People talk in shouts and there is much banter back and forth between tables and between those at tables and those at the bar. Card playing is often accompanied by loud table slapping and as the *tute* games progress, the calling of trump or the counting of points is accompanied by various curses, more vulgarisms than obscenities. A group of soldiers home on leave may insist on loudly singing marching and other songs. Only when there is some important program on the television will the other customers insist that they quiet down, which they always do without argument.

Important television programs are generally entertainment programs such as *Noche de Sabado,* a popular variety show. Bullfights are televised and the crowd in the bar responds much the same way as they would if actually present. Some American shows have been dubbed in Spanish and have become popular in Spain. It is not only the entertaining or the spectacular that attracts the viewer. Spanish television regularly presents classics of Spanish theater: once an entire bar full of gnarled farmers and *resineros* in a hamlet near El Pinar watched a production of "Don Juan Tenorio." The bar was completely silent as the men followed the plot and the silence was broken only when some of the more famous passages were delivered; men who hadn't been to school for forty years or more found themselves repeating the lines that they had once memorized as schoolboys, like a Greek chorus accompanying the television actors.

Villagers are forever inviting friends to a glass of wine or wine and soda. Also they drink much coffee in the evening as well as various glasses of cognac. For all the drinking, it is rare to see a drunk man, although many of the young men will get "high" after an evening of making the rounds of the bars. People do not drink to get drunk; rather the offering and taking of beverages is part and parcel of the whole ritual of friendly social relations and is an expected part of daily life.

Reciprocity is observed in the village; one does not accept a *chato* without offering to buy the next one. Usually drinks are bought in a round so that each member of the group takes a turn paying. This is not always explicit; guests are often exempted from the duty. It is not an onerous duty but rather a general expectation that sooner or later one will reciprocate. The same applies to cigarettes; they are always offered to others and it is unthinkable to light up before having offered the pack around to everyone.

Refusal of a drink or a cigarette can be delicate since refusal may imply an insult. The egalitarian ethic is strong in the village and, while social differences are noted by the people, they do not like to have them made more visible by rebuffs. To offer a man a drink or a cigarette is symbolically to offer him friendship and good feeling, and one must learn how to be both a good host *and* a good guest. It is simple to refuse a cigarette if one doesn't smoke; a simple "I don't smoke" will suffice. The same holds true for liquor. Actually, among friends, a simple "no thanks" does the job; it is the newly met people or in situations where there is a marked social distinction between the parties that refusals must be couched in very diplomatic terms to avoid offense.

The same general ethic prevails when one enters a person's home. Even the closest friends and relatives will knock on the door and inquire *"¿Se puede?"*— (Can I come in). If eating, they offer the visitor food which is ritually refused by saying *"que aproveche"* (may it be enjoyable for you). Normally the host will insist that the visitor have something and will bring out some cookies and a glass of anise liquor or cognac as a gesture of hospitality.

While the distinguished guest will be ushered into the parlor, the family and old friends spend their time in the kitchen, especially in the winter months when it is the only warm room in the house. Much of the family life goes on in the kitchen, meals are usually eaten there, and it is no accident that the term *hogar,* the old style open kitchen fireplace, is also used for home. Kitchen gatherings are informal and are the scene for card games, gossip, and passing time.

For a few days each year, the village seems to come alive. Holidays such as Christmas and Easter and the fiesta in honor of the village's patron saint, St. Anthony of Padua, are occasions for reunions when distant family members return home for visits with kinfolk and friends. Most Spanish holidays have a religious base but while solemn masses are sung in the churches, it is the secular attractions that spark the gaiety and festive atmosphere of the *pueblo.* Each year, the fiesta is planned by a committee of the village council and, except for bull-fights where an admission fee is charged, villagers attend soccer matches, handball games, dances, band concerts, and fireworks displays without charge, the expenses being borne by the village government. For five days the normally quiet village is alive with noise and excite-ment while the villagers and visitors from neighboring pueblos gather, mostly in the Plaza, to participate in what is nominally a celebration in honor of a saint.

The actual beginning of the fiesta is on June 3rd when the Novena in honor of San Antonio commences, ending in a vesper service and Rosary service the evening of the 12th. However, the real gaiety begins after the Rosary when, at 8:30 P.M., the band marches through the streets playing gay *pasodobles* and followed by the *gigantes* and *cabe-zudos,* these being paper mache heads of various historical or fanciful figures worn by village men. The *gigantes* are over ten feet tall and are heads and long robes erected on a frame which can be carried by one man. Invariably, these figures represent Ferdinand and Isabela—the Catholic Sovereigns. The *Cabezudos* are large paper-maché heads worn by men gowned in appropriate robes. The village children run in mock terror from them while the older boys throw firecrackers at the robed figures and the official fireworks "artist"—a local man who does the job every year—shoots off skyrockets to the general delight of all.

After the band has toured the main streets, it returns to the Plaza where dancing goes on until two in the morning. Often there is an-other dance going on in the dance hall at the same time and, while an admission fee is charged, it is small and keeps no one away.

The streets to one side and behind the church become a carnival midway, with various booths where anyone may try to win a prize by shooting a pellet gun at targets, by throwing a ball at milk bottles (made of wood), or buying a raffle ticket on some item from a variety of carnival people who make their living going from village to village following the fiestas.

The bars are full. Families wander from bar to bar, there are loud greetings exchanged between neighbors and friends, and even strangers will soon be adopted by some wandering group if they show even the minimum signs of being friendly. In every bar there will be the same types of groups; old men playing cards just as they do every day, a group of young soldiers singing marching songs and looking bedraggled in their heavy wool uniforms, a group of mature married adults engaged in conversation, little children playing on the floor, and groups of self-conscious teenage girls trying to get the boys to look at them so they can snub them in the time honored Spanish fashion. This scene is repeated every night during the fiesta.

On the 13th the band and the *cabezudos* and *gigantes* parade through the streets at 9 A.M., awakening the town with music. Since this is the Saint's day, a Solemn High Mass is celebrated in the church at noon. For this occasion a visiting priest gives the sermon in praise of the Patron. The Mass is crowded and, for once, some semblance of solemnity is observed as the village officials and the members of the *cofradias* (religious brotherhoods) file in in procession and sit near the alter.

Immediately after the Mass comes the procession through the village. The statue of San Antonio is placed upon a litter decked with flowers and carried by four men preceded by the band and followed by the municipal authorities and one of the priests. Since the procession lasts three hours, the priests take turns in line. This is the liveliest of all the religiously based activities. Instead of hymns, the band plays the gay *jota,* long the typical folk dance of the area. While both men and women may carry the Saint's statue, only men may dance the *jota* in front of him. The band plays the *jota,* the men and boys dance, and as the music ends everyone shouts, *Viva El Santo!* and *Jota!* The dance is done in two lines, each man with a partner facing him, and as time and the sun wear down their endurance, partners drop out and new men enter the line. There is no limit on how many may dance at once. Coats and ties soon come off and the men dance on as the band perspires freely but gamely plays urged on by the shouts of *Jota!*

At the end of the three hours, the statue is returned to the church but is not allowed to enter without a dispute. The band, the municipal authorities, and the priest are all importuned to let the dancing continue and young men block the church doors with their bodies to prohibit the Saint from entering. While this is going on, a number of people will silently come to the statue and lay money at its feet. This is money given the Church in return for the Saint having aided them through some crisis during the year and is given as fulfillment of a vow.

The origins of dancing before the Saint's image are obscure and debatable, but the custom is generally held to be for the purpose of expressing joy and enthusiasm for the Saint and thanks for his aid. In 1967 the wheat harvest was so abundant that all the farmers collectively vowed to dance as a sign of thanksgiving for the bounty given them by God through the intercession of San Antonio.

The rest of the day is devoted to dancing and to sporting contests such as a bicycle race and a handball tournament.

On the 14th comes the bullfight. El Pinar has a long tradition of staging first class *corridas* and the event attracts people from the surrounding villages. Normally village bullfights are conducted in a makeshift arena composed of farm carts and the *toreros* are novices trying to break into the profession.[2] In El Pinar, the *corrida* is almost always a bullfight with young apprentice *toreros* who will soon become full matadors and who fight decent bulls with the full company of assistants including picadors. In 1967 El Pinar actually held a bullfight with first rank matadors—an event that attracted the attention of the national press. For these *corridas,* the arena is not made of farm carts but is a portable set of stands rented from a company in Barcelona.

The next day, the 15th, the youth have their fling at bullfighting. A *becerrada* is organized; this is an event in which yearling bulls are used and anybody with a rag to wave can get in the arena and get knocked over and/or gored. A professional *torero* is always in charge of this event, but while he is supposed to kill the bull, usually he is doubled up with laughter most of the time like the rest of the crowd.

The fiesta of San Antonio ends on the night of the 15th or, to be more accurate, sometime in the small hours of the morning of the 16th. The day after the fiesta sees the town almost desolate as everybody who can catches up on lost sleep. The pitchmen take down their booths, the itinerant candy sellers load their trucks or wagons, the soldiers leave for their bases, and things quiet down again until next year, except for the discussion and post-mortem as to whether this year's fiesta was as good as last year's or that of some earlier era.

For the folklorist, the fiesta will be a disappointment. No traditional

---

[2] An excellent account of small village bullfights and aspiring toreros is given in Collins and Lapierre's biography of "El Cordobes" (1968).

Fiesta. An innovation in the 1969 fiesta was floats, such as this with a "princess" and her attendants. The traditional "gigante" representing King Ferdinand "the Catholic" follows.

costumes are worn and the music is more often standard pop and rock and roll than folk tunes. One recent innovation is the parade of floats constructed by various groups of young people and modeled after American events, such as the Tournament of Roses and Cotton Bowl parade which have been shown on Spanish television. There has been talk of electing a "Miss El Pinar" in the future. These innovations seem to please the older people who recall the days when the fiestas were far less elaborate; none seem eager to return to the older traditional celebrations, although they do exhibit a certain nostalgia for the simpler celebrations of their youth.

The fiesta is for everybody and everybody participates but not to the same extent. The elderly people come to look at the festivities in the Plaza and generally leave early to go to bed at their customary hour. Housewives, especially those with house guests, have to devote a great deal of time to cooking and housework and appear only in the evenings for the dances. Since the fiesta falls at approximately the same time as the barley harvest, farmers cannot attend all events. They and the *resineros* try to do only the most essential chores during the five day period. There is no pressure to attend or participate in the fiesta, and while most people do attend, a few find the noise and crowds so distasteful that they make a deliberate effort to avoid the Plaza. No one thinks any the worse of them for this.

The fiestas in the El Pinar area are not occasions for great extravagances or conspicuous consumption. A few former villagers who live and work in cities do show off their new affluence by wearing their best clothes and buying rounds of the best cognac for friends, but they are regarded as fools by the average villager who wears his regular dress clothes and who may make a gesture of extravagance for the occasion by buying a good cigar instead of a cheap one. Conspicuous consumption and violence, often characteristic of Latin American fiestas, are virtually unheard of in rural Spain.

The essence of the fiesta is a sort of combination of a regular Saturday night and Sunday morning with some extra attractions thrown in. There is a certain sameness to the people's behavior: people visit each other in homes and in bars, the conversations are on the same topics as usual, the young people sing and dance as they usually do, and the weekly *paseo* is repeated on a daily basis. Behind the carnival atmosphere, the fiesta is basically an *intensification* of behavior appropriate on other days when celebration is in order. While most people feel good, there is no evidence that any higher degree of community solidarity or social integration is brought about by the fiesta. And after it is all over, El Pinar returns to the dull grind of work which is its everyday life and waits for the next holiday which will be celebrated essentially like the last.

The Economy

Most literature dealing with the economy of Spain is macro-economic in scope in that it tends to deal with the national economy as a whole or with specific major sectors such as tourism, agriculture, etc. Somewhere in the mass of statistics is the economic microcosm of El Pinar. Although the typical villager is unsophisticated in economic theory, he is aware that his livelihood depends upon forces and conditions not always of his own making and that his fate is inextricably linked with that of his nation.

At the end of the 1936-1939 Civil War Spain was in a state of economic chaos. Some 250,000 homes had been destroyed and an equal number partially damaged. Roads and railroads were almost entirely wiped out, the Merchant Marine lost 225,000 tons of shipping, and the nation's gold reserves, sent by the Republican government to Russia for safekeeping, never returned to Madrid. These figures meant little to the peasants in the villages. To them, the War meant fewer jobs, lower pay, no secure working conditions, and hunger.

One of the main characteristics of the internal Spanish economy of the 1940's was the existence of a "Black Market" for both necessary and luxury goods. The Postal Agent in El Pinar earned 15 *pesetas* a day in 1949, an income from which he had to support a family of ten, an impossibility since his wages would not even cover the cost of bread alone. Like most of the townspeople, he and his family eked out a supplementary income through farming and odd jobs on the side. In 1949 the cost of living was 5 times as high as in 1939, but the salaries were only 2 ½ times as high.

Farm prices were also very low during the 1940's. The fixed price for wheat paid by the government was 0.86 *pesetas* a kilogram, hardly enough to allow the farmer to recoup the costs of seeds and machinery, let alone labor costs. What happened is widely known in Spain: farmers held back some of their wheat for sale on the Black Market where they would get a higher price, tax figures were falsified as were production figures, and nearly everybody looked out for his own interests first.

The decade of the 1950's brought considerable improvements to the Spanish economy. Foreign investments increased, and the treaty made by the Eisenhower administration setting up a Navy base at Rota and

Air bases at Zaragoza, Torrejon, and Moron de la Frontera brought in not only American dollars but a certain amount of prestige and international recognition to the Regime. (While the economic impact of the bases was great, the opinion of some Americans that this treaty saved both the economy and the government from collapse is seen by Spaniards as a gross exaggeration.) Industrial and agricultural production expanded, and while the cost of living rose steadily, more consumer goods were available. The Black Market went out of existence and salaries also rose somewhat.

As the general economic conditions improved and levels of living were raised, goods and services once considered luxuries became so widely available that soon they were thought necessities. The increased meat consumption in El Pinar is an example. In 1949 chicken was a luxury, in 1966 it was a common item on the table and those few who could not afford chicken considered themselves, and were considered by others, to be in poor condition.

The attitudes of the people of El Pinar relative to the economy are rather simplistic: if they have more money than before, things are good; if not, things are bad. The industrial expansion in Valencia, or the harvest in what was once a desert in Badajoz, or Spain's future in the Common Market is irrelevant; the local view is essentially a short-range view. Although aware that he is at the mercy of an international market in, for example, wheat and resin products, the average villager does not understand fully how these markets operate. What he does understand is the amount of *pesetas* he has in his pocket, in his bank account, or sewed into his mattress. The rest is of little significance to him.

The general economic conditions of the Province of Segovia can be summed up as poor. Compared to the other 49 provinces, Segovia consistently ranks near the bottom on most economic indices.

The basic factor influencing this condition is the overwhelmingly agricultural nature of the Province. In 1960 47.71% of the Gross Provincial Product was produced by the agricultural sector (excluding forestry) and most of this production was dry farming of cereal grains. In that same year the active agricultural population of the Province represented 56.76% of the total labor force and 21.34% of the total population. Only about 12% were employed by industry and commerce.

In agriculture as in industry, the basic problem is the *minifundio* (small scale exploitation). Most farmers are small self-employed own-

ers or renters who rarely hire farm help, and in industry the situation
is analogous.

According to the classification system used by the *Banco Español de
Credito,* El Pinar ranked in Class 4, the least important class for towns
in the 1,000 to 3,000 population category. Class 4 is described as:

. . . municipalities which possess a commercial value which is practically nil
or which is essentially based upon the acquisition of the most common
products of a low unit cost, thus constituting a strong indicator of self-suffi-
ciency which characterizes the greater part of the rural Spanish zones.
(BANESTO, 1966: 80-81)

The most difficult figures to get are those relating to income; not because of a lack of cooperation, but rather because few people keep accurate (if any) records and because of the variety of type of income
found in any one family. For example, a refinery employee may receive, in addition to his wages, income from a garden plot, income
from eggs sold by his wife, rent from a house he owns, and money sent
home by a daughter working in France. The same holds true for self-
employed farmers, *resineros,* and small shop owners.

As a group, the *resineros* are in the best condition with an estimated
annual income of 75,000 *pesetas.* However, as resin product prices
were falling, their position was becoming more precarious.

The *resineros* generally work a 9 month year, from March to November, and all the farmers likewise cease most activities during the
coldest winter months, December through February. This seasonal
work stoppage is typical of the El Pinar area. During this period,
there are some public works projects such as road repairs, as well as a
few weeks of work trimming the pines and cutting down "condemned"
trees. Except for some chores or occasional odd jobs, most agricultural
workers are unemployed at least three months out of the year.

The major industry in El Pinar, excluding agriculture, is the production of resin and wood products, the major industrialist being
Eusibio Moreno. Together with his family he owns pine lands, farms,
factories, and properties all over Spain; they are generally considered
to be one of the wealthier families in the country with an income well
up into millions of *pesetas* each year. Most of the salaried workers in
El Pinar work for one of Moreno's enterprises, and most of them are
unhappy about their low wages. The average refinery or saw mill
worker takes home about 4,000 pesetas a month. The base pay is 90
pesetas a day, plus extra pay depending upon the number of depen-
dents a worker has.

The employment situation in El Pinar is poor. There is no demand for workers, a situation that goes back to at least 1963. It must be added that this lack of demand is common throughout the rural area of Segovia. This does not mean that no need exists; Manolo, for example, had to cut down on the amount of land he was farming since he had no help except an occasional hand from his wife and brother-in-law during the harvest. What it means is that the farmers do not wish to spend the money, or do not have the money, for temporary workers. Also, there are very few people in town willing to work on a temporary basis. There are about 15 such "casual" workers in town. Most of these are either returned emigrants who have enough money to live on and are just interested in picking up a few pesetas until they return to France or Germany or young men of 21 going into military service and who are killing time until their reporting date.

Many townspeople criticized Eusibio for not "doing more for the town," *i.e.*, not expanding production, creating new jobs, and raising wages. In all fairness, it must be noted that few Spanish businessmen, especially in rural areas, are accustomed to "doing something for the town," and the general attitude of workers and employers alike is essentially, "take care of yourself first."

Actually, some work is always available in El Pinar, but it is usually only temporary, and always poorly paid. For this reason, most young men and many young women choose to emigrate permanently to the urban industrial centers or temporarily to France and Germany, where one may earn as much in four months as in a year in Spain. One case, somewhat exceptional, was Ramon who spent 90 days in Germany painting steeples and smokestacks and netted 40,000 *pesetas* for his work. Most migrants abroad make less than this, but in general they are able to earn more than in Spain.

The lack of well-paid employment, the low profit yield of agricultural products, declining value of resin products, and the need to emigrate presents a fairly bleak picture, especially to the youth. In comparing today's conditions with those of a not so distant past, the older people are almost completely agreed that life has never been better. More people are earning more money, everybody has plenty to eat, housing is generally in good condition, and nobody lacks the extra *pesetas* to treat his friends to a drink, to attend a movie, or to purchase some of the smaller luxuries of life. The younger people are far less content and most try to find a more remunerative livelihood in the cities.

The public sector of the economy presents a fairly good appearance on the surface; in reality, the *pueblo's* financial conditions are in a state of decline. El Pinar generally has been considered by both residents and people of other towns as being "rich." The paved streets, the new school, the sewerage system, etc., are tangible evidences of municipal wealth, and there are few towns in the area of the Province which can boast of equal or superior facilities. Most of the money for construction of these facilities was provided by the Provincial or National governments, although the City Hall had to put up part of the funds for initial construction and has to pay most of the maintenance and operating costs.

Residents of El Pinar pay no municipal taxes for the services received, and there is no record of their ever having to pay such taxes. The village government provides a somewhat sporadic street cleaning service, pays two *serenos* (night guards), and provides the usual administrative services of record keeping, etc., this latter service sometimes requiring the payment of small fees, five or ten *pesetas,* but more often provided without charge. The police services of the *Guardia Civil* are paid for by higher echelon governmental bodies, as are the salaries of the schoolteachers and the priest. The citizens do pay taxes on income and property but these are paid to the Provincial or National governments and not to the municipality. In certain situations, the people are charged for some services. The priest is paid for weddings, funerals, and special masses. Parents pay fees to the schoolteachers for private classes leading to the *Bachiller Elemental* and *Bachiller Superior* diplomas or for private tutoring sessions. In addition, there are fees for shotgun licenses, bicycle permits, and the like, most of these fees going to the Province or to some national Ministry.

The funds from which the local government must meet local expenses come from the municipal patrimony, the pines and some pasture land. Each year, these lands are leased out on a competitive bid basis to individuals or companies wishing to tap the pine trees or graze livestock on the pasture lands. The funds gained from these leases provide about 97% of the total municipal income, excluding appropriations from the governmental bodies which are accounted for separately and do not figure in the local annual budget.

The basic economic problems in the public sector of the municipal economy stem from the steady decline in income from the pines due to resin prices, falling because of competition from lower priced synthetics.

The simple fact is that the municipal economy of El Pinar is dependent upon the income from the pine leases. The pines have been the mainstay of the economy for well over a hundred years and most people in town cannot conceive of the possibility that someday these pines might be practically worthless. The only alternatives seen by the people were the levying of municipal taxes to pay for the services or increased governmental aid in the form of a large scale irrigation project to transform the dry lands into more productive and better paying lands. In the first case, nobody is enthusiastic about paying local taxes. The general prediction is that such a move would cause a large scale emigration to the cities and ultimately the death of the *pueblo*. Taxes are high enough according to the people, and there is also the question of "on what are we supposed to pay taxes?"; a logical question, granted the low profit margin of the farmers. The second alternative is dismissed out of hand by most people. Although there are periodic reports in the press about large scale governmental aid to agriculture, most people feel that the national government is more interested in industry, and furthermore, that any aid would be given to other provinces. Segovia was considered as being forgotten "in Madrid."

The people of El Pinar discount the possibility of private enterprise as a means of bringing about radical economic improvements. Only Eusibio Moreno had enough money to do this, according to the general populace, and he wasn't about to do anything. The only hope was that "someone with a lot of money" would build an industry in the town but everybody agreed that this was unrealistic and there are no efforts being made by the community to attract outside investment capital.

Some of the wealthier farmers did diversify. One balanced his wheat farming with a large herd of beef cattle. The San Miguels converted part of their factory to the raising of chickens, and even Moreno diversified by manufacturing door and window frames in one of his plants. These efforts, however, affected only the private sector; all the municipal authorities could do was join in with authorities from Leyes, Villa Roman, and other pine oriented towns to petition the Civil Governor for help. In the long run, the only solution with any hope of success lay in asking "the State" to do something.

Despite their hopes and their well known resilience in the face of hard times, the people of El Pinar are not all optimistic about the future. About half the town thought that El Pinar would survive, even if the population probably would shrink to the old people and those farmers who had enough land to maintain a decent living. The most expressive means of showing an opinion is that of the youth; about 75% "vote with their feet," heading for a brighter and more secure

future in Madrid or Bilbao, or, on a less permanent basis, to France or
Germany.

What was a decent income in El Pinar in 1967? That is, how much
must a family earn to be able to have a house, dress, and eat moderately
well, and afford some of the smaller luxuries of life? The question was
put to the young people, who were less apt to tolerate some of the conditions their parents are accustomed to. The general consensus is that
50,000 *pesetas* a year would allow one to "live well" in the *pueblo*. An
income of 120,000 *pesetas* yearly allows one to live very well, even allowing for ownership of a car and a television set—two of the most
prized luxury items in Spain.

"Living well" is an essentially subjective judgement. Hence, in El
Pinar, many people said they lived well by their own standards although objectively it was clear that some people had more and better
material possessions than others. Actually, the mere possession of material goods is not the sole indicator of how well a person lives. The
people in El Pinar include in their judgement such variables as health
and "tranquility," which are not amenable to precise measurement.
This is not to say that material goods do not matter. Don Juan, who
was Municipal Secretary until his transfer in 1966, made the flat as-
sertion that the goal of every young Spaniard was the possession of an
automobile. Cars and television sets have a status value apart from any
utilitarian value. I found no contradictory evidence in talking to the
young people but the interest of the boys in owning a car was somewhat higher than that of the girls.

The elevation of the level of living in Spain and the changing consumption patterns can be noted in one small segment of the economy
—the shoe repair shops. Since 1960, 35% of these establishments have
disappeared in Spain. The reason is fairly simple; having more income, people can buy more shoes. Formerly it was common to wear
the same pair of shoes during both summer and winter; now many
people buy summer shoes which last only one season and are not repaired. As a consequence winter shoes are worn less and thus need
fewer repairs.

Most men in El Pinar have at least two pairs of work shoes and two
pairs for dress use; the women are apt to have more. Prices are not
particularly low, a good pair of women's dress shoes may cost 800
pesetas and an average pair of work boots for a man, 350. Yet the shoe
stores in Segovia have frequent sales and offer discounts, and a wise
shopper can get bargains frequently. Ten years ago shoes would be repaired frequently. Today even the frequency of half-soling, the most

common repair next to new heels, has declined 40% from the 1960
level.

The same general situation exists with clothing. The people of El
Pinar dress well on Sundays and holidays or on special occasions, the
men in suits and the women in stylish dresses and accessories. Patched
clothing is used for work and not for dress occasions. There is a definite
social value in dressing well and both the quality and the quantity of
clothing reflects the new prosperity. A good hand crafted suit with two
pair of trousers costs 3,000 *pesetas* in Segovia, an overcoat from 1,500
pesetas to 2,300 and a white shirt of an artificial fiber 300 *pesetas*. The
women buy cloth and either sew their own garments or have them made
by one of the local seamstresses or a talented friend. At these prices, there
are few who cannot afford a new suit or coat at least every three years.

While the main source of municipal income is threatened, personal
income has risen and more people have more personal possessions
than ever before. The older people are relatively happy with the new
prosperity and the youth have at least a hope of achieving an economically secure future, even if it must be outside the village. But
while there is an attitude of cautious hope, most villagers realize that
the economic viability of El Pinar, and villages like it, is still very
much in doubt, and few are willing to look to the village's future with
any great optimism.

CHAPTER IV

Being a Villager

To BETTER UNDERSTAND the people of El Pinar and their reactions when faced with change, it is necessary to have some understanding of their basic values. People everywhere are most likely to accept innovations when these do not conflict with traditional values and beliefs satisfactory to them. Among the various definitions of the term "values", I prefer that offered by Kenny:

... a series of conceptions from which a preferred type of conduct is evolved and imposed by the social system; which can be abstracted by analysis but which may not be consciously recognized or verbalized by every member of society. (1961-62 :280)

Honor And Shame

Two of the most widely known aspects of Spanish character are the related values of honor and shame. According to Peristiany (1966:11), honor and shame are constant preoccupations in small and exclusive societies where primary rather than secondary relations are most important, and where a man's personality is as significant as the social position he holds in the society. The Spanish village provides precisely this type of social setting, where, as Pitt-Rivers has noted, honor is both the person's estimation of his own worth and his claim to pride as well as the acknowledgement of his fellows to his right to that self-conception and pride. (1966:21)

The entire topic of honor in Spain has been well discussed by Pitt-Rivers, (1963). A summary of the basic nature of honor in Spain is given in *Honour And Shame* (1966) edited by Peristiany. The topic also has been extensively treated by Spanish authors for at least several centuries in both scientific and popular literature.

In El Pinar as in all Spanish villages, a person's reputation in the community is based upon his honor and that of his family. A good reputation is essential if the person is to survive socially in the village. An honorable man exhibits certain traits. He is *serio* (serious) and *formal* (dignified) in his dealings with others, yet at the same time he is *simpático* (friendly). Kenny sees being *simpático* as a communicative device. It is having ". . . the art of knowing *how* to be in touch with another person as well as knowing that one *is* in touch with him." (1965: 80). The essence of the outward expression of honor is poise—the honorable man is a poised man in dealings with others regardless of class or social position.

Another aspect of honor is the conviction that one is just as good in a moral sense as any other man—it is an egalitarian ethic that does not regard high socio-economic status as a determinant of, or a necessary condition for, the attainment and possession of honor. Thus, every villager feels himself to be at least the moral equal of every other man regardless of his income, education, or occupation.

Honor, for the man, is related to the concept of *hombria* (manliness) which is not to be confused with the phenomenon of *machismo* supposedly common in Latin America. In Spain, manliness is not judged by the sexual proclivities and conquests. To be manly it is necessary to exhibit courage in the face of danger and adversity in a poised manner. One of the ideals of this sort of courage is found in the bullfighter who faces death with a tranquil countenance and even with a smile. A man's bravery is often praised by the vulgar expression that he has *cojones* ("balls"). Juxtaposing behavioral traits with bodily parts, bravery comes from the testicles, as passion comes from the heart.

Unlike the more verbally expressive peoples of Andalusia studied by Pitt-Rivers, the Castillian villager does not often speak of honor unless challenged by another. Then, the challenged must decide how to vindicate his honor if, indeed, he feels the challenge worthy of answer.

The most serious challenge to a man's honor is to insinuate that he is a cuckold by referring to him as a *cabron*. The term literally means he-goat and is so odious that even he-goats of the four legged variety are referred to as *cabritos*, the diminuitive form of the proper noun *cabra*. This insult, not peculiar to Spain, is widespread in the Mediterranean areas of Europe from Portugal to Greece.

Directly related to honor is the concept of shame, which can be described as a lack of honor brought about by a loss of honor. The term *sin vergüenza*, shameless, refers to the dishonest, the immoral, and to neer-do-wells in general.

To be *sin vergüenza* in the community is to be beyond the
pale of decent life and decent people. The shameless person will
not be trusted, he or she may be insulted almost at will and does
not have the right to retaliate. Nor would his or her retaliatory
words have much effect since no one would pay any attention to a
dishonorable person.

Vergüenza is of critical importance for women, who are expected
to be above reproach especially insofar as sexual activities are concerned.
The ideal role model for the woman is the Virgin Mary—the *Im-
maculada* or Immaculate One. Premarital sexual intercourse is prohibited and if a woman is known to have indulged in such behavior she and her family are dishonored. The family honor may be
restored by disowning the girl; this may mollify the community but
the sense of shame felt by the parents and near relatives may endure
many years.

An impression of immorality or promiscuity is sufficient for a girl
to be known as shameless if she has done nothing wrong. One of the
more tragic cases was that of a young girl in her twenties known
locally as "Frenchy". The daughter of a once hard working man
who had become the village drunkard, "Frenchy" went several times
to France as a migrant worker and adopted mannerisms unacceptable
to the village. She dyed her hair blonde and usually wore dresses
cut too low for the approval of the village women. One memorable
summer day, she went swimming in the river wearing a bikini—
attire that only recently has become acceptable for middle-class and
upper-class girls and then only at beach resorts. When "Frenchy"
walked back to town in that bikini, the tongues of the village
women wagged for many hours and the comments of the men were
no more gentle.

During a Sunday evening dance, "Frenchy" showed up by herself—
a not altogether unusual act since only formally engaged couples
come together and most of the young men and women come alone
or in small groups. Not one of the young men would dance with
her. All of the men were sexually experienced—a fringe benefit
of their previous employment in France—and there were remarks
about the possible abilities of "Frenchy" in that sphere of activity.
This in itself was unusual since village boys are usually reticent
about making comments of a gross sexual nature about local girls,
since these same girls are probably close relatives of their friends
and to insult the honor of a friend is not done—at least not while

the friend is around. I suggested to several of the men that they dance with "Frenchy", but they refused, stating that they would not be seen publicily associated with her. Since she was regarded as shameless, none of the men wish to have anything to do with her for fear of later being rebuffed by decent girls, as well as out of a desire not to embarrass their families by being seen with a girl whose reputation in the village was, to put it mildly, bad. Even men who knew that "Frenchy" was not immoral in any real way shied away from her out of fear of an implacable public opinion that had branded her as shameless and thus beyond the pale of decent folk. This was the last village dance "Frenchy" attended; after several weeks of social isolation she returned to France to stay, there being no hope for a normal social life for her in El Pinar.

Both honor and shame are intimately linked with ideas of morality which are legitimated by both sacred (*i.e.* Church) and secular norms as to the nature of propriety in behavior. In general, the code is a strict one. Yet, there is evidence that the mores are changing to some extent. The courtship pattern described by the Prices for an Andalusian village (1966) is essentially the same pattern followed in El Pinar. None of the girls under 30 recall chaperones and that venerable Spanish institution, the *dueña*, has been in disuse for at least 40 years in El Pinar. Less formal methods of social control serve to keep deviations to a minimum.

One married woman noted that it was not uncommon for girls to deliberately get themselves pregnant by their fiancé so that they would have to get married; this was usually done as a final way of overcoming parental objections to the marriage. This type of behavior was not unusual during the 1940's but it is rare today. In sexual matters, the Spanish girl is most moral although there is an old proverb that states: "*Entraron en el bosque dos y salieron tres*"— "they entered the forest as two and came out three."

Loss of *vergüenza* is not strictly limited to sexual impropriety. A shameless person, male or female, can achieve that status by lying, cheating, stealing, refusing to live up to reasonable family obligations, or by any improper presentation of self in public.

The major agency of social control is not the law, but that seemingly omnipresent group known as "they". In Spain, it is phrased as *¿que dirán?*— "What will they say?". While many people say that they do not concern themselves with what the public will say or think, nevertheless they do because a dishonored person cannot expect to live a good life in the village.

The Good Life

Living a good life implies having certain material benefits and a sufficient income as well as the possession of non-material things such as health and tranquility.

As far as the material benefits are concerned, there is a rising expectation in the entire *comarca* as there is, indeed, in all of Spain. Good clothing is highly prized; the typical Spaniard likes to dress well, sartorial elegance is highly valued. But these things cost money as do the other material things such as television sets and automobiles.

The good life includes good health. Illness is commonplace in peasant societies, due to poor nutrition and to lack of medical care. In the El Pinar region people are generally in good health and medical services are quite good. Diets are not well balanced from a nutritional point of view, and people complain about the high fees charged by the village physician, but most people are relatively healthy and eat well. The environmental health conditions have been vastly improved since 1955, which is important inasmuch as the people recognize that no good life can be led in an unsanitary environment.

The burning desire of farmers, *resineros,* merchants, craftsmen, and all others in the village is to make more money and do less work. This statement in essence sums up what, in material terms, the villagers meant by the good life.

Family

The major social unit to which each individual belongs is the nuclear family. While the nuclear family is the basic unit, close ties are maintained with brothers and sisters living in the village as well as with aunts and uncles and, to a lesser degree, with cousins.

Kinship is the closest association a person has to others. Ideally, close relationships exist between parents and children and between siblings. Close relationships also exist between grandparents and grandchildren and between uncles and aunts and their nieces and nephews. The relations are usually close, which does not necessarily mean that they are always friendly; intra-family quarrels are common.

Close relationships usually exist between first cousins. Second and subsequent cousins are people with whom one may or may not have close relations, depending upon individuals and circumstances.

The term *pariente* (kinsman) is used as a blanket term to include all relatives but usually refers in practice to those beyond the level of first cousin or immediate affines. *Parientes* use the informal *tu* in speaking to each other instead of the *usted* form reserved for strangers and superiors. Criteria for determining one's *parientes* are loose. In one case, one of my *parientes* claimed the relation on the grounds that my paternal grandmother's sister's husband was somehow related to his wife's family. The utility of the term is that it is most flexible and does not bind one to any specific duties such as the duties of a father to a son. Since village endogamy is common, almost everyone is a *pariente* to everyone else.

In El Pinar the addage that "blood is thicker than water" has great social meaning and high value is placed upon loyalty to family. Unfortunately, the norm of loyalty is often violated and intra-family squabbles are common, especially when property and inheritance matters are at stake. However, in good times and bad, it is to the family that the individual must rally. The sense of strong family solidarity that various writers have described in southern Italy does not exist in the same degree in El Pinar. While present to some extent, the stress upon the family as a corporate entity has declined since the Civil War, due in part to dispersion of the children through emigration away from the parental home in the village.

Tranquility And Individualism

Honor, shame, and family have been extensively discussed in the literature on Mediterranean Europe and especially Spain. Little attention has been paid to the high value placed upon *tranquilidad* (tranquility). All classes, age groups, and both sexes seem unanimously agreed upon the need for peace and order and the avoidance of trouble.

Tranquility is achieved by avoidance behavior; that is, one is tranquil if he avoids trouble. The phrase *meterse en líos* literally translated means to "place oneself into trouble". Trouble is viewed as being always present and latent in every social situation; it is inherent in the social system. Thus, one achieves tranquility by role behavior designed to avoid troublesome relationships. One achieves tranquility with one's fellows by not engaging in any behavior which may activate the troubles always latent in human interaction. The formality, dignified bearing, and often elaborate language and social rituals in part can be understood as a set of devices designed to minimize potential conflict. The Castillian peasant is not the so-called "volatile Latin"; he is a very rational, cautious, and prudent man, and frequently a very worried one.

Individualism is frequently expressed by the phrase *"Hago lo que me de la gana"* (I'll do that which I feel like doing). It assumes an individual's inalienable right to do as he pleases but with the implied obligation that his actions do not seriously interfere with the rights of his fellows to do likewise.

Egoismo and *personalismo*—selfishness and personalism—are aspects of the general value of individualism which have been accepted by both Spanish and foreign writers as being an integral part of the Spanish character structure. When Don Eugenio told me that "this village is the enemy of cooperation", he was referring to the individualism of the villagers which was assumed to preclude any long-term cooperative efforts.

This facet of Castillian character has been grossly exaggerated in the literature and by the people themselves. The expression of highly individualistic and idiosyncratic behavior is limited to relatively in-consequential acts, such as singing at the top of one's voice in the Plaza at 2 A.M. because one feels like it. In matters affecting the family and in relations with others, the villager is restricted by local norms and a rigid set of social controls. The rampant individualist runs the risk of punitive action by family and associates and the further risk of not being regarded as *serio* and therefore not to be trusted in serious adult affairs.

The people recognize that much of the cherished freedom of in-dividual action can be expressed and acted out only within very narrow limits. A person is free to sing out in the Plaza—up to a point. He can debate the merits of a given bullfighter or soccer team—to a point. The point is reached when he infringes upon the presumed rights of others or becomes such a nuisance that others will demand he calm down. Individual expressions about the more serious matters of religion, politics, and community affairs are generally avoided in public. This is not so much out of any fear of reprisal by the authorities but is more a reflection that the person is aware that his ideas and expressions may activate the troubles always latent in the social milieu.

The values of individualism and tranquility are, to a great extent, mutually exclusive in a small village. One cannot be in-dividualistic and have tranquility at the same time. The villager realizes that much of his individualism in only an illusory and highly problematical potential which can never be fully realized. Any unbridled or unseemly individualistic actions where others are involved raises the spectre of *líos* (troubles) and the subsequent threat of the loss of tranquility.

Religion

Old Castile is regarded as one of the most conservative areas in a religiously conservative country. Churches, shrines, priests, processions, and other outward manifestations of Roman Catholicism abound in Spain, and El Pinar is no exception. Yet there is growing evidence that the fervor of the faithful is slowly declining, especially in the urban areas, and this may be taking place in the small villages as well.

Most of the people of El Pinar—indeed the overwhelming majority—regularly attend Mass on Sundays and Holy Days of Obligation; men and women attend in approximately equal numbers. Religion is taught in the schools and is supported by the State in many ways. Yet, there is a curious indifference among many of the villages to much of traditional Catholicism and this is most noticeable among young people. The village priest expressed his opinion that devotion in El Pinar was satisfactory although he frequently, in his sermons, excoriated the people for their sins.

The power and control over the people by village priests is rapidly declining all over Spain. Young Spanish clergymen are being profoundly influenced by the liberalization of Church dogmas and practices brought about by the papacy of John XXIII and the Vatican Councils. Many, such as Don Sebastian the 26 year old assistant priest in Leyes, support the idea of separation of Church and State. The 1967 Religious Liberty Law which granted freedom of worship privileges to non-Catholics reflected what the younger clergy and most of the laity had felt for some time. While the most radical Church-based social action programs, such as the worker-priest movement, are confined to large industrial areas like Barcelona and Bilbao, the impact of these programs is being felt in the rural areas as newly ordained priests take their initial posts in the small villages.

In one village Don Jose, a newly ordained priest, was assigned to assist the regular parish priest, a man in his seventies. The older priest more or less ignored the younger man, who apart from saying Mass and hearing confessions, had little to do. The older priest, a conservative, saw to it that he did not preach any sermons on reform and social justice. Having time on his hands, Don Jose began visiting the bars and talking to the young people, taking an interest in their problems. What he did was most unusual—he went to the people instead of waiting for them to come to him as his superior customarily did. On a few occasions he took youth groups on trips to fiestas in the area, often wearing secular garb instead of the traditional cassock. The young people, most of whom attended Mass more out of habit than out of desire, developed a new respect for their Church. Even the older people praised the young priest for his attempts to help their children and by their praise effectively stopped the senior priest's attempts to stifle his hitherto unheard of activities.

Kenny, in his account of Ramosierra (1961), stresses the integrative functions of the *cofradias*—lay brotherhoods dedicated to the veneration of a particular saint. *Cofradias* exist in El Pinar; the *cofradia* venerating San Antonio for men and the *Hijas de Maria* venerating the Virgin Mary for women are the most important ones, though their integrative functions are minimal. Members meet only once a year for a religious ceremony and procession; otherwise individual members go their own separate ways, and some are not even on speaking terms with their brother members.

One cannot ignore the potential role of the Church as an integrative organization in a community, but the amount of actual integration depends to a great extent upon the personality of the priest. A man like Don Jose or Don Sebastian can do a great deal to bring people together, while a man like El Pinar's resident priest, Don Eugenio, cannot. In discussing resistance by the villagers to forming cooperatives, one agent of the *Servicio de Extensión Agrária* (Agricultural Extension Service) who knew the village well suggested that getting a new priest would be a giant step forward in improving agriculture.

Education

For the past five years primary and secondary schools in Spain have been implementing a series of changes designed to upgrade curriculum and facilities and improve the quality of teachers. While elementary schooling is available without charge to all, only about 60% of the children enrolled in the El Pinar school complete studies for the *Bachiller Elemental*, an educational level approximately equivalent to 9th grade in the United States. Thus, of the 308 primary students in 1969, only about 185 would finish elementary school. Of these, about 50 would enroll for secondary education leading to the *Bachiller Superior*.

Secondary education is supposed to be available at no charge to parents, but in practice special tutoring fees must be paid to the teachers to prepare pupils for the comprehensive examinations required as part of the secondary education program.

Education is the main avenue for upward social mobility. A person without at least some formal education will have difficulty in getting a job in Spain's tight labor market and will probably be doomed to do low paying manual labor for the rest of his life. While most of the villagers realize this and desire a good education for their children, many fathers discourage secondary schooling for their sons since they need the boys as workers on their farms or in their businesses. In many cases, children leave elementary school at the age of eleven or twelve to work and thus bring in sorely needed income to the family. Fewer girls than boys attempt secondary schooling and the drop-out rate is higher among the female students. Since the destiny of girls is, with few exceptions, that of being a housewife, there is little desire on the part of parents to spend money for an education they deem of little practical utility. In addition to this, girls often discontinue their studies in order to aid their mothers at home or to go to work.

Despite the high drop-out rate of students and the desire of many parents to have their children gainfully employed, the people of El Pinar place a high value on education. People who had little schooling as children try to insure that their children take advantage of educational opportunities they never had. Their support of education is not based upon the value of intellectual enlightenment but rather because good schooling pays off in aiding a person to secure a better job.

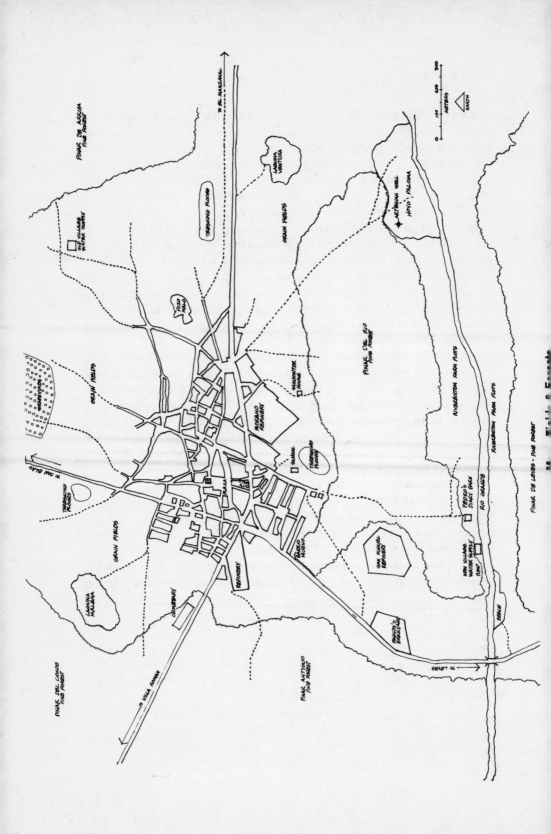

CHAPTER V

Forests and Fields

The Pines

SPAIN AT ONE TIME was so heavily covered with forests that, according to legend, a squirrel could travel from Gibraltar to the Pyrénées without ever having to set foot upon the ground. Today, of the 26.8 million hectares of woodland remaining, less than one-third is high dense forest, and three-fifths consists of scrub wasteland and eroding hillsides. The Province of Segovia, especially in the area of El Pinar, is one of the major regions producing resin for naval stores. Whatever municipal wealth the villages of the *comarca* receives comes primarily from the extraction of resin from the *pinus pinaster*, the resinous pine that grows in the area. In the 1840's the village was producing tar, turpentine, and resin derivatives in small refineries and the major wealth of the village came from its trees—although the majority of the populace were engaged in farming.

The *pinus pinaster* is a slow growing tree. It take approximately forty years for the average tree to achieve the minimum diameter it must have before being tapped for resin. Once having achieved the legal minimum, the tree is tapped for a ten year period, lies fallow another five or ten years, and then goes back into productivity for ten more years. Thus worked, each tree has a productive life of about 60 years. By the time a tree reaches 100 years of age, it is usually "condemned to death," chopped down, and the wood used for lumber or for firewood, according to quality.

The traditional system of extracting the raw gum is the so-called *"uve"* system. Using a curved cutting tool on a wooden handle, the *resinero*, having previously shaved the bark where the face cut is to go, makes a face cut of about 12 centimeters in width at the base of the tree. A metal gutter is inserted into a cut in the tree below the face to guide the flowing gum into a ceramic cup. Each tree is worked with one face which, after five years, usually reaches about seven feet above the base where it started. A new face is then started at the base of the tree. Trees "condemned to death" are worked with two or more faces during their last year of productivity.

The *resinero* using the *"uve"* system normally visits each tree every five days, when he makes a fresh cut at the top of the face with a semicircular motion. Three or four swift scrapes are made in a matter of a few seconds by a skilled *resinero*. It is a deceptively simple looking operation, but one that requires strong arms and shoulders and a great deal of care by the person so as not to hack up the tree. As he makes his daily rounds, the *resinero* empties the filled cups into barrels, which are then picked up when full, and taken to the refinery.

The normal resinero works an allotment of 4,000 trees, which, allowing for "condemned" trees, gives him about 4,500 faces to work. From this number of faces, he gathers about seven barrels of gum every twenty-five days. Practically all the *resineros* in the village work communally owned pines; a few also have some private pine lots which rarely exceed 500 trees. The resination season extends from the first of March to about the end of October, and thus, the *resinero's* employment is a seasonal one.

Forestry in Spain is a strictly controlled enterprise subject to very rigid government regulation. No *resinero* may begin work, even on a private lot, until the official opening of the season as decreed by the *Distrito Forestal* (Forest District) in Segovia. Face cuts must not exceed legal limits of width and depth, and no tree may be tapped for the first time until approval by the proper authorities has been given. No tree may be cut down without approval, and even the gathering of firewood by the villagers is regulated.

In the old days—the early part of this century—one of the major events in the village was the arrival of the Royal Forest Engineer from Madrid. This personage was an awesome gentlemen who appeared riding an elegant horse and whose very word was absolute law. It was he who decided which trees would be "condemned to death," which new areas of the forest could be opened to cutting, and woe to anyone who dared his word. My father and others of his generation well remembered him and old *resineros* tell how his very look could freeze a man. The normal supervision of the forests was the domain of Tio Ventura, the Forest Guard who died in 1937. Well known and loved in the *comarca,* he had the final say on forest utilization as the representative accountable to the Royal Engineer.

Today, while the Guardia Civil patrol the forest, the direct supervision and care of the trees is left to the special Forest Guards who take their orders from the *Distrito Forestal.* Actually, the need for rigid supervision is minimal; the villagers of the *comarca* are very much aware of the value of the pines and little policing is really necessary.

The Communidad

Excluding privately owned plots, the vast majority of the pines are owned by nine villages jointly known as the *Communidad de la Villa y Tierra de Villa Roman.* These *Communidades* originated in medieval times and usually consisted of the *Villa,* which was the seat of the ruling lord, and a number of settlements known as *lugares* (places). The *Communidad* was a form of organization, very prevalent in Old Castile, with rights and privileges of its own. Even Isabella had to swear to uphold the rights of the various *Communidades* in Segovia prior to her being crowned Queen of Castile in that city.

As some of the power of the medieval lords began to wane, or as various *lugares* became wealthier or more powerful, the inevitable splits and schisms developed and some of the *lugares* became *municipios* (municipalities) and claimed portions of what was once land communally held by all *lugares* of the *Communidad.* In the case of Villa Roman, we know from local records that its earliest government was an *Alcaldia*—a Mayor and Council. Later, in the 15th and 16th centuries, a noble family exercised feudal dominion over the *Communidad.*

The struggle for independent status by the various *lugares* who wished to follow the example of similar entities in Leon and become *municipios* began in the 16th century. A Royal Order by Felipe II in 1583 set forth the rights of the *Communidad* of Villa Roman and rejected the pleas of the *lugares* who wished to close off communal lands for their private use. Similar decrees in 1585, 1623, 1664 and up through the 19th century had little effect and gradually the *lugares* achieved status as *municipios* but remained confederated into a *Communidad* in most cases.

The *Communidad* of Villa Roman today includes El Pinar and Villa Roman as the two major towns, plus seven smaller villages.

Each village is a separate political entity, but the *Communidad* owns most of the pines as well as some pasture land. The major purpose of its existence is to distribute income from the community property among the member *municipios* proportionately according to their populations and to make rules regarding forest and land usage. Since other government agencies now control conservation practices and regulate land utilization, in effect the *Communidad* does nothing. This is the view from El Pinar; the authorities in Villa Roman would disagree since, after all, their village is the seat of the *Communidad*.

As might be suspected, the division of lands and the profits realized from the pines has been the source of arguments and lawsuits between the villages involved. Excerpts from correspondence in the El Pinar City Hall may give some insight into the character of the people as well as the problems of administering the pines. The chief complaint was that Villa Roman was taking an unjust share of the proceeds and not giving a fair accounting of the yearly receipts.

In a letter to the *Diputación Provincial* (Provincial Assembly) dated 12 December 1873, the villagers of El Pinar complained:

... we must present various of the abuses which Villa Roman has been committing in the distribution of benefits to which we have equal rights—such as the firing of some employees and naming others in their place as has taken place recently with the forest guards and about which we have already written you.

If Villa Roman, Dear Sir, had lived up to its word and obligation, we would not have to bother you again, but some time has passed, and more than enough for them to have done something about this matter.

In December of the same year, the Mayors of San Juan and Leyes also registered a protest to the *Diputation:*

It is necessary to make the City Hall of Villa Roman understand that for some time the right to abuse their companions of the *Communidad* has disappeared, and fortunately, these odious privileges will never reappear again. The *pueblos* are going forward to their regeneration and strong in their rights to do so. The *pueblos* of the *Communidad de Villa Roman* have rights to intervene and be represented in their administration.

Part of the problem stemmed from the fact that the ruling *Alcadia* of the *Communidad* consisted of the Mayor of Villa Roman, and his Council. Three representatives from the remaining group of villages were entitled to participate in the decisions regarding the distribution of profits, but either they were kept out of the meetings, did not attend, or were bribed. The records give no indication of what actually happened.

El Pinar took the issue to court and in 1906 obtained a judgement ordering the authorities of Villa Roman to exhibit the records of the pine income. The order was not complied with, and the village of El Pinar continued to lead the fight. A Madrid lawyer was brought in to handle the plaintiff's case in 1927; two more lawyers were hired in 1929. The petitions went on: in 1927, El Pinar appealed directly to the *Ministerio de Gobernación* (Home Ministry) in Madrid:

We are, all of us, sons of Villa Roman, but now emancipated and with the ability and duty to regulate our lives and house freely without any tutelage from Villa Roman.

The laws of 1583 governing the *Communidad* can no longer apply. The *Communidades'* laws were suppressed by Royal Order on 31 May 1837, and furthermore the *Communidad* must come under the general provisions of Article 91 of the *Ley Municipal* of 20 August 1870 and the similar law of 1871.

(The) *Communidad* which produces annually more than 300,000 *pesetas* of income distributes only some 120,000 and in spite of its importance, only the City Hall of Villa Roman and the three *interventores* which represent more than 7,000 inhabitants know the actual income which makes this discrepancy so important. The *interventores* have paid no attention to this situation, nor has the City Hall; all claim a complete ignorance of the matter—conduct which has been going on for some fifty years or more. This can be seen by the complaint of San Juan of 25 December 1880.

Noting that the bad feelings between El Pinar and Villa Roman went back to at least 1872, the petitioners in another document addressed to the same Ministry cited the addition of insult to injury:

Among the abuses most outstanding which we believe the City Hall of the *Villa y Tierra de Villa Roman* has committed is the case of their present construction of a *Casa Consistorial* (Town Hall)—completely sumptious— with funds from the *Communidad*.

The Civil War of 1936-1939 brought an end to the squabbling, although dissatisfaction still continued. There was never any open fighting or armed conflict between *resineros* of the different contending villages.

Today the profits apparently are divided amicably and justly between the member villages of the *Communidad,* and Villa Roman has not been accused of any chicanery. However, Villa Roman does profit by its position as the seat of the *Communidad* and its municipal authorities have tended to use the prestige of this position to the advantage of their village.

While the pines are owned communally, each village is alloted a section for the use of its *resineros*. To avoid being stuck with unproductive pines for life, each *resinero* works a plot of trees for a five year period and then receives a new plot. This allocation is done by a lottery drawing.[1] Any resident of a village may choose to be a *resinero* but a system of seniority assures that the established *resineros* have first option in the lottery. Depending upon the number of trees open for exploitation, some men may go without trees for a season; in other seasons, there may be a shortage of *resineros*. Generally speaking, this problem is not an acute one as all the established *resineros* usually receive a plot of trees each season.

Each year prior to the opening of the resin season the villages of the *Communidad* offer their sections of the forests up for lease at a sealed bid auction. The bids are open and competitive, but in El Pinar the bid is usually won by the Moreno refinery with some areas being taken by the San Miguels. The *"Resinera"* in Villa Roman usually picks up the bid for the pines in the Villa Roman and Leyes area. In announcing the auction, the villages state the number of trees available, their location, and the minimum acceptable offer.

The Crisis of 1967

During the 1967 season a crisis long brewing struck the *comarca*. Resin prices had fallen off sharply due to increasing costs of production. Also, Spain was finding it difficult to compete with foreign countries, notably the United States and, to a lesser degree, Portugal. Many of the *resineros* were impressed—albeit a bit ruefully—to learn that the United States alone produced over half of the world's naval stores supply. The crisis came as a rude shock to the villages; for centuries they had depended upon the pines and the people found it hard to believe that their most valuable treasure was fast becoming worthless.

During the 1966-67 resination season, each *resinero* received three *pesetas* per kilogram of raw gum that he extracted. Falling prices made it uneconomical for the refineries to pay the price for the raw gum since, after processing and marketing the derivatives, their profit

---

[1] A roughly similar situation exists in Ramosierra (*cf.* Kenny, 1961) although the ownership basis of the trees differs from El Pinar.

margin would be so slim it would make their work unprofitable. In February of 1967 the problem was brought up to the highest levels of government and a temporary solution reached. A *resinero* would receive 3.75 *pesetas* per kilo of raw gum plus a one-time supplemental payment of one *peseta* per tree. This price would be subsidized by the national government.

When the first auctions in the *comarca* were held, no bidders could be found. The villages lowered the asking price in a second auction and, again, no bidders responded. The third round of auctions lowered the prices still further and all pine lots offered were finally leased by the usual companies.

The effect on the villages can be measured by a few statistics included in a special report made by the Civil Governor of Segovia. The *Communidad's* income for 1967 from the pines (including timber) was expected to be 4,822,109 *pesetas,* but the amount necessary to maintain the forest would be 5,307,213 *pesetas*—a clear deficit of 485,104 *pesetas.* Furthermore, income from the pines in the Province had declined from 71.4 million *pesetas* in 1961 to 23.8 million in 1966.

The seriousness of the situation became a matter of headlines in the *Adelantado de Segovia,* the provincial daily newspaper, during February and March. Citing the Civil Governor's report, the paper noted on 11 February 1967 that the following consequences could be expected unless something was done: eighty three villages would be economically ruined, 19 refineries would be forced to close, 107,000 hectares of otherwise useless land would have to be abandoned, 2,000 workers would become unemployed, and it would be necessary to import naval stores at a cost of 3.2 million dollars to meet the national needs for the products. Various solutions were proposed. Refiners insisted that municipalities and *Communidades* lower their taxes on corporations; for example, the *Communidad* levied a 12.36% tax on income received by the refineries leasing *Communidad* pines.

On 29 February 1967, the day before the official opening of the resin season, it appeared that 10 *resineros* in El Pinar would be without trees due to the refusal of the *Distrito Forestal* to open up one area for resination. The fact that the following year would see the new section opened and a subsequent shortage of *resineros* did not mollify the men; the ten *resineros* and their families would have to emigrate if they were to survive.

That morning the Mayor of El Pinar, a simple farmer and politically unsophisticated, and the Municipal Secretary drove to Villa

Roman for a conference with the Mayor there, a protegé of a high
official in Segovia and a shrewd politician. He further had the advantage of knowing something about pine economics, having
previously been a clerk for a large refinery. Arturo, the Mayor of
Villa Roman had assumed the role of spokesman for the villages of
the *comarca* in the pine crisis; it was he who made the speeches in
Segovia, and who, through the intercession of his highly placed
patron, got the concessions for the *Communidad*. He was a man who
dedicated his life to the wellbeing of the *Communidad*; he took the
problems of all the villages as seriously as he took those of his own.
He was always quick to point this out. Nobody really believed him,
of course.

El Pinar annually produces more resin than Villa Roman, but
neither the Morenos nor the San Miguels are politically a match for
the Villa Roman authorities. Thus, the *resineros* of El Pinar felt
that they were being forced to suffer because of the machinations
of the Villa Roman politicians and the "don't give a damn" attitude
of the industrialists of their own village.

The Mayor had a problem on his hands. A few nights before the
El Pinar *resineros* had banded together in an unprecedented way and
swore that as long as every *resinero* had trees, they would all work.
But if the ten men were not given trees, none of them would work.
Some of the *resineros* of Villa Roman then said that they would move
to take over the trees left deserted, but the men of El Pinar let it
be known that they were prepared to use their cutting tools on
something besides trees. The matter was discussed by El Pinar and
Villa Roman authorities and ultimately brought to the attention
of the Civil Governor who obviously used his power to solve the
problem. On the 9th of March, the *resineros* all had pines to work
and the threatened work stoppage never occurred.

New Resination Techniques

One of the key economic factors involved in the low profit yield
of the pines is that they have very limited value for lumber. The
pinaster pine is not a tall erect tree and has little value for poles.
Also, the series of faces carved into the sides of the pine damage the
wood and cut down the useable portion of the cut log. Unless ways
could be found to increase the lumber utility of the trees and lower
the per-kilogram unit cost of extracting the resin, the economic decline of the *Communidad* was assured.

To achieve these ends, a number of major technological changes were in the process of introduction in the pine areas of the Province. The "Pinar Antiguo"—a forest lying between Villa Roman and El Pinar was something of a model forest for experimental techniques. A Forestry Training School had been established in 1959 at Villa Roman to train *capataces* in forest management. These men took one year courses at the school and did practice work in conservation in the area woods. During summers, forestry students from the University of Madrid underwent practical field training in the same area.

Formerly, the woods were clogged by low bushes and underbrush which often choked off new seedlings. The older trees often crowded each other for space, with the result that many of them became twisted and gnarled. While still useable for resin, their lumber value was minimal. A series of conservation regulations went into effect during the decade of the 1950's; the underbrush was cleared away and, in some areas, the land was plowed or harrowed. Fire breaks had always existed, but the new clearing policy reduced even further the danger of forest fires. A new reforestation program was implemented vigorously.

The major technological change in resin production came in 1967 with the introduction of a new system of cutting known as the *pico a corteza* system. This involved the use of diluted sulphuric acid applied to the face. It was the first major technological change in the memory of the oldest *resineros* insofar as the pines were concerned, and the manner of its production to the area and its reception by the *resineros* is an example of how innovations were brought about among this supposedly traditionalist people.

In January 1967 two young men arrived in El Pinar. Luis and Manuel were "Monitors" of the *Promocion Professional Obrera* agency of the Labor Ministry. The PPO was organized in 1964 for the purpose of training workers for new skilled jobs to be created as part of the First Development Plan and to upgrade skills of workers in certain existing jobs. The Monitors were young men with special technical training and a good amount of zeal and enthusiasm for their mission. The PPO team of two or more Monitors was assigned to a village to conduct courses for varying durations for the workers, usually in the evening hours when the village men returned from their normal work. Enrollment was voluntary and while the PPO provided the necessary equipment for teaching and demonstration, the students received no pay or other aid while attending the course.

Around the end of November 1966 it was rumored about the

Young resinero *Julian Sanz*, demonstrates use of acid resination technique. Scar on tree's right is an old "face" worked for five years with the traditional "uve" cutting method.

village that a PPO team was coming to El Pinar to teach a course in chain-saw operations. New rumors then had it that a new resination technique would be taught by the same team. Actually, the PPO teams had been asked for by the City Hall and the rumors were just slightly distorted versions of true facts.

Extracting resin by the *pico a corteza* method was not unknown in El Pinar. Cayo, one of the *resineros*, had learned the technique while employed as a *resinero* in the Province of Albacete and had begun to use the new technique on a small lot of pines which his family owned. The other *resineros* of El Pinar had seen his trees but were divided in their opinions of the utility of the new process; none of them adopted it or even experimented with it except one *resinero* who had about 100 trees of his own. Indeed, the *resineros* were rather skeptical of the new process and they feared that the acid would ruin the wood of the tree. Also, the use of the technique on *Communidad* trees would require approval of the *Distrito Forestal*, and such approval had never been either solicited or given.

Luis and Manuel appeared in the village one day with their PPO panel truck and took up rooms at the inn operated by one of the bars. Then, for a period of two weeks, they did little but hang around the village meeting the people informally. They stated their purpose for being there and announced that they would be offering the new resination course. Their approach was part of a calculated effort. Once having made the necessary courtesy calls upon the Mayor and local authorities, the monitors just hung around, playing cards in the bars, chatting with the men, and making sure that they knew the people. Subtly, they piqued the interest of the *resineros*, but made no attempt to force on them the new technique. Both monitors were very emphatic on one point: they were primarily interested in changing attitudes first. Had they arrived and immediately set up classes, no *resinero* would have attended; their approach was strictly soft-sell.

During this period, Luis and Manuel walked about the woods talking with *resineros*; they looked into the refineries, and very quickly became a normal sight in the village. By the time the course began, all the *resineros* were talking about the new technique. Some of the younger ones, like Mariano Salamanca and Cayo, who had used the technique on their own pines, were enthusiastic. The older *resineros* were less enthusiastic and some of them went to great lengths to ridicule the innovation. But Luis and Manuel had studied their men; when the first class of 57 *resineros* assembled, they knew each man and his attitude.

The *pico a corteza* technique involves making a small rectangular face cut on the tree using a different type tool than the one used in the *"uve"* system. A set of new tools would cost the *resinero* about 500 *pesetas*, a price that was very inexpensive since the tools would last for years if well cared for. The main innovation was the use of acid.[2] Once the face was prepared, a mixture of 50% sulphuric acid and 50% water would be applied at the top of the face cut from a plastic squeeze bottle with a long spout. In warmer months, the mixture was 45% acid, and in the hottest months of July and August, 50% acid. Ideally, distilled water was to be used but regular water was generally used with no significant reduction of efficiency. Using the new technique, the face would be treated every eight days instead of every five, meaning a man could work more trees. The acid cost 80 *pesetas* a liter and this would provide a solution good for 40,000 applications.

The system has one drawback. Even though the acid produces heat which aids in the extraction of the gum, the gum flow is slower in the cold months when the work begins, and only later does the flow increase beyond the normal. Thus, the *resinero* has to wait longer for his money since he is paid by the refineries upon delivery of his barrels. This is not an insuperable difficulty since most *resineros* can hold out until the higher yields begin.

The chief objection of the *resineros* was that the wood could be damaged by the acid. They had seen the burn scars on Cayo's trees and were fearful of permanent damage to their trees. The Monitors explained that Cayo was using the technique incorrectly; after all, he had never had any formal training with it. Cayo readily admitted this, although he claimed that none of his trees were damaged and his yield not adversely affected. In a delicate situation where he could have lost face among his colleagues, he managed to save his pride, because, after all, he had been the first to know of the technique, even if he wasn't too perfect in its application.

What the *resineros* wanted was essentially more money with less work. The Monitors could not promise a higher yield of gum; indeed, the acid technique does not increase yield from a tree. However, it was an easier way of working the trees, and this appealed to the *resineros*. Classes stressed application and practice with a small amount of theory

[2] This technique is widely used in the southeastern United States. It appears to have been introduced into Spain around 1959 by Spanish forestry engineers who had studied the technique in the United States.

thrown in. Some of the *resineros* had a "complex" about showing their ignorance in class, but tactful handling by the Monitors resolved most of these problems. Once convinced that the trees would not be damaged and that the new system had merit, the *resineros* began to learn in earnest. The classes were held each evening for about two hours in one room of the old school in the City Hall. Men, many of whom had not set foot in a classroom for forty years, came to learn, and there were no dropouts.

At the end of the course, the men received diplomas from the PPO. There was a celebration with free beer and food and speeches by the Mayor and the Provincial Delegate of the Labor Ministry who came from Segovia for the occasion. However, the *resineros* were still evaluating the new techniques. Five or six were determined to use it immediately but most wanted to think it over or experiment with a few trees to see how the results would be. During the summer of 1969 only about 20% of the trees were being worked with the new technique, partially because approval for its use had not been given by the *Districto Forestal* for all pine lots and partially because a number of the *resineros* did not like the acid because it spilled on them and burned holes in their clothes. The idea of the new technology had been almost universally accepted, but implementation was going slowly because many of the *resineros* realized that their income would not be substantially increased by use of the acid technique and this was to them the most important factor in judging the innovation.

Agriculture

El Pinar lies in a poor soil area that is basically a very sandy loam with areas of clay base; officially, the soil is classified by the government as "mediocre" for farming purposes. Annual rainfall is scanty; over the last 60 years the area has received an annual rainfall of approximately 700 millimeters. Most rain falls during the spring and winter months, although late spring and early summer thunderstorms often bring hail which destroys the crops. The basic water sources are the two rivers which pass by the western and northeastern edges of the village territory and wells and springs which provide water for both domestic and farm use.

The basic agricultural pattern is dry farming with fields being rotated on the *año y vez* (alternate years) system. Barley and winter wheat are planted in the fall and harvested in the summer. Grapes are harvested in October and sugar beets, a new crop, are harvested in winter. The traditional crops grown in the area have been winter

Directed by a "monitor" of the P.P.O. (in suit), a resinero demonstrates his proficiency in use of a chain saw, as villagers look on.

Fast disappearing in El Pinar are the high wheeled farm carts drawn by oxen.

wheat, barley, melons, pumpkins, grapes, carob beans, lentils and chickpeas. These are produced by dry farming techniques on the high plains which comprises most of the village's farmland.

Fall plowing is done with the traditional Roman plow with a chisel point. A few farmers use mold-board plows but the chisel is most efficient for the sandy loam soil which is often baked hard by the intense summer heat. Grain seeds are hand broadcast after the plowing and the fields are weeded by hand hoes during the growing season as the situation demands.

The traditional fertilizer used in the area prior to the advent of chemical fertilizer was animal manure, usually from sheep. In some parts of the *comarca* sheep are kept out in the unused fields in portable wooden pens which are moved every evening to a new site. In this way, the animal dung is deposited over the land serving to fertilize it. Some farmers also use manure from cattle, mules, oxen, and burros which they collect in compost heaps in their corrals and then transport to the fields. In the El Pinar area, this practice has been slowly declining since 1955.

Barley is harvested toward the end of May and the wheat harvest traditionally begins around the 25th of July, the fiesta of Santiago— patron saint of Spain. Procedures for harvesting both crops are essentially similar and can be described in general as a repetition of similar techniques.

The earliest form of harvesting was done by handle sickles or scythes; the grain stalks were gathered into a small bundle by the farmer and cut off near the ground. This method was in use in El Pinar in 1949 but today has almost entirely been replaced by machinery. However, there are still wandering groups of *Gallegos*— migrants from the poorer areas of Galicia—who work in some of the villages and harvest grain by this hand method.

The most common form of harvesting machinery is a mule drawn harvester with a fixed cutting blade and four wooden sweeps. The grain is cut by the blade and thence swept onto a pan where it is pushed off onto the ground. Workers follow the machine and gather up the bundles of grain, using smooth curved sticks to aid them in scooping up the bundles. The bundles are tied, often with a cord made of a special kind of wheat grown for its unusually long stalks, and left in the field.

Once the farmer has harvested and bundled his grain, it is transported in the two wheeled farm cart to the *era* (threshing floor). In El Pinar the *eras* are located on three sites near the edges of the village. The threshing floors are hardpacked dirt and, aside from sweeping them clean, no special preparation of them is required.

The wheat or barley, as the case may be, is piled into a huge mound and a number of bundles are untied and the grain with the stalk is placed in a circle on the *era*. Threshing is carried out by a wooden threshing sledge, a device virtually unchanged since its introduction by the Romans over 2,000 years ago. The sledge is made of wooden planks bound together by iron straps, and its bottom is inset with sharp flint stones. Most sledges weigh approximately 200 pounds and are about five feet long and three to four feet wide. The sledge is hitched to a draft animal, usually a mule, although oxen were used in the past and are still used in the poorer villages, and the farmer stands on the sledge and drives it in circles over the grain.

A common task of threshing is usually assigned to one of the farmer's young sons or helpers. He carries a bucket or can and waits for the draft animal to raise its tail; at that point he holds the container so as to prevent fecal matter from falling onto the grain. If the animal urinates, there is nothing the farmer can do. No health hazard is involved since subsequent milling operations cleanse the grain and the flour, but many of the farmers good-naturedly attribute the fine taste of local bread to its high "organic" content.

While the farmer may wait until all his wheat has been threshed, usually his family or his helpers will begin the second phase of the operation as soon as enough grain is ready. As the sledge continues its rounds, a helper will winnow the grain. Using special three or four tined wooden pitchforks made from one piece of wood, he will throw the grain into the air so that the breeze will separate it from the lighter chaff. The clean grain is scooped up and placed into a separate pile. Once most of the chaff has been separated by winnowing, it is placed in a grain cleaning machine, usually operated by a hand-turned crank. Grain and chaff are separated; usually the process is repeated twice to achieve the desired degree of cleanliness and separation. Then the grain in placed in burlap sacks and transported to the farmer's corral for later shipment to the *Servicio Nacional de Cereales* granary in Leyes. The chaff and straw are taken to his corral for use as animal fodder or as bedding for pig or cattle stalls.

Chickpeas, lentils, carob beans, and melons are harvested by hand-picking; cleaning and shelling is done by the farmer's wife and daughters. Most of these crops are grown for home consumption or for very limited sale within the village and they can be regarded more

Tractor-drawn combine rented in Leyes harvests wheat. Note how the grain fields run right up to the edge of the pine forests.

as subsistence crops than as cash crops, although a few farmers make a profit from them.

Grapes in the El Pinar area are both of the red and white varieties. Sevogia is not a major wine producing area and grape production has declined markedly as more and more of the land has gone into grain production. However, most villagers, including many non-farmers, have small plots of grapevines, the grapes being used in part for making wine for home consumption and, to a lesser extent, for eating.

The *vendimia* (grape harvest) was, at one time, a major festival in the rural area but has declined to insignificance. By local law and custom, guards are elected by the farmers and paid by the City Hall. They are posted as the grapes begin to mature and are supposed to insure that no one begins to harvest grapes earlier than the date set by the municipal authorities. Also, they are supposed to prevent thefts of grapes. It is a standing joke in the village that the guard posts go usually to men who are deaf, blind, dumb, and preferably crippled. When the grapes are ready for picking, the City Hall announces the date and gives official permission. Men, women and children go out to the plots and gather up the grapes in baskets which are then emptied into farm carts. The old technique of crushing grapes by foot has given way to the grape press. Wine is made by the family in its corral and stored in a *bodega* (winecellar) in bottles or large jars. Often a large pigskin whose interior is coated with tar is used to hold several hundred liters of wine; this primitive but effective storage device is even used by large commerical wineries in other regions of Spain to transport wine to the cities and villages. With red Valdepeñas wine available at six *pesetas* a liter and the tart, acid Rioja wines at about the same price, there is little economic incentive to grow grapes on a commerical scale in the El Pinar area. Indeed, many farmers take no care of their vineyards, being content to pick whatever grows each year until they plow the vines under and use the land for new crops.

Irrigation

Irrigation is relatively new in the El Pinar area, even along the river bottom lands of the two rivers which flow by the village. This is due in part to the topography of the land; the nearer river lies in a deep gorge with some narrow bottomland that is fertile enough not to require irrigation. The Rio Chico, smaller of the two, lies at the extreme edge of the village lands—some seven kilometers away.

One measure of the extent of irrigation can be noted by the fact that of all arable land in the village in 1963, 1846 hectares were dry farmed and only 30 hectares were irrigated. This proportion has changed little since that time—perhaps another 30 hectares have been brought under irrigation. In El Manzanal, to the east, the picture is similar: 2364 hectares are dry farmed and only 10.5 are irrigated. Villa Roman has 65 of its 237 hectares irrigated, but this village has little agriculture and much of the farmland is in a river bottom area. Leyes, while far from the river, has a higher water table and is also a more modern village, and 1933 hectares are dry farmed and 500 irrigated, with more irrigation canals under construction.

In El Pinar the most intensive riverine agriculture is along the bottomlands of the Rio Grande. Prior to the Civil War most of this land was used for vegetables. Today most of this bottom land produces a variety of garden crops such as tomatoes, beets, various vegetables, alfalfa, and some corn and tobacco.

The original irrigation systems seem to have been small canals dug from the edge of the river to nearby fields. A number of springs in the area also supplied water. There is some dispute as to the use of the *noria* in the El Pinar area; according to informants these came into general use around 1912. Of the many *noria* sites, only three or four are in use today. Another form of raising water from a well is the *cigüeñal*. The *cigüeñal* is a bucket attached to a long pole, counterweighted on one end, and fixed between two upright support beams. Only a few of these are still in use.

In the Hoyo Paloma area, a wide valley near the Rio Grande, an artesian well provides a fine source of water for irrigation. The well is capped and a small pump attached, allowing for greater control of water volume. This most fertile area in El Pinar is the property of two families. At one time wheat was grown there, but this was discontinued in the 1940's.

On the upland plateau area, which is where most farmers have most of their land, there is little irrigation. There are some wells and water sources, especially in the northeastern quadrant of the village area, and a few scattered wells elsewhere. Some old *noria* sites exist and a few *norias* are still operated sporadically. Until the installation of a modern pumping system on the Rio Grande in 1962, the village drinking water came from a water source in the hills northeast of the village, about a kilometer from the village itself.

During 1966 there was one major attempt at irrigating an upland farm plot. Five farmers pooled their land for the production of sugar beets, a crop that needs much water. A small gasoline motor pump drew the water from the Rio Chico, about three kilometers from the plot, into a retaining pond. The pond, or reservoir, was built of cement blocks. A tractor was used to provide power for suction to fill up the reservoir, and the same tractor could provide power for the sprinkler irrigation system in use. All piping was lightweight aluminum, including the sprinkler pipes which were moved about the plot as needed.

Prior to approximately 1955 there were, near the village, several small ponds, which were used for watering livestock but were not for irrigation nor as sources for drinking water. Most ponds were filled when the village physician decided they were a hazard to public health since they were breeding spots for mosquitos and other insects. At one time Pozo Malo, one of these ponds, was stocked with small fish which were gathered up by the pond's owner in the fall as the pond dried up. Another pond was used as a site for the making of adobes. The few remaining ponds today have little use beyond service as livestock watering places or as likely spots for hunters waiting to shoot doves or other game birds during the season.

Some villagers maintain small garden plots on the outskirts of town or, in a few cases, in their own corrals; these are devoted to the production of lettuce, tomatoes, and similar garden truck for home consumption. A few people, such as old Pablo, a retired *resinero*, sell their produce in the village as a source of supplementary income. At least one man tapped into the water main before its junction with his house water meter and was having a very successful garden in the corral as a result.

New Crops

Most farmers are using improved hybrid seed for their wheat and barley, as well as for other vegetable crops and melons. But the major new crops are sugar beets and tobacco. Sugar cane is grown in a few areas of Southern Spain and has never provided enough sugar to support national demand. Partly to meet the national demand, and partly to give the Castillian farmer a more diversified crop base, sugar beets were introduced into the area around 1955. The advantage of the crop lies in its ready marketability and its relatively good price. It is simple to grow, requires minimal equipment, and the sugar refinery provides the seed at low cost.

Sugar beets were readily accepted by the farmers of the *comarca*.

Manolo and his wife gather up cut wheat into sheaves. Note the flat curved stick which is used to aid in scooping the loosely piled wheat into a bundle, which is then tied.

There were several reasons for this: first, many men had worked in France in the sugar beet areas and were familiar with the crop; secondly, the crop was profitable and provided a source of income during the winter months when it was harvested. Unlike the French farms, there is little mechanization in sugar beet production in El Pinar, the planting, weeding, and harvesting being done largely by hand.

Most who accepted the crop planted it in plots near the river bottoms, especially near the Rio Chico.

The second new crop introduced into the *comarca* was tobacco, the so-called "black" variety commonly used in Spanish cigarettes. Tobacco requires far more care than sugar beets but the economic rewards are much higher and there are no acreage allotments nor restrictions on production. Some men from the village were taken by the Agricultural Extension agents to Talavera de la Reina in Toledo, where the government maintains a demonstration area for new crops, and there they saw tobacco growing and became interested.

Tobacco seed was procured with government aid; a number of farmers planted the crop and the first year brought successful harvest. Seven tobacco drying sheds were built in El Pinar; these were brick buildings of considerable size to allow for the open air curring of the leaf. The second year the crop was attacked by the Blue Mosaic plague which destroyed most of the plants. No remedy for the plague could be found and, except for a very few small plots, tobacco is not longer grown in the *comarca*. The drying sheds were converted to other uses, some became cattlebarns, other became storage places, and a few just remain empty and unused.

While the crop failed, the enthusiasm of the farmers did not. Failure was due to natural causes understandable to all farmers and they would gladly resume growing tobacco if a cure of the Blue Mosaic plague were found.

Mechanized agriculture

Despite his supposed traditionalism, the Castillian farmer has a very high regard for sophisticated farm machinery and an equally high desire to possess such machinery. While more and more farm machinery is being used in Spain, the bulk of the planting, harvesting, transporting, and processing operations are performed by manual or animal labor since the high cost of machinery precludes its purchase or rental by most farmers.

The simple mule-drawn grain harvester used by Manolo and many other farmers cost 15,000 pesetas in 1962—a not inconsiderable sum for men whose annual income barely approached 60,000 pesetas. When Manolo first saw one of the machines he did not understand it, but once he saw the advantages it would bring him, he went ahead and made the purchase. The advantage was clear: no longer would he have to harvest grain with a hand sickle and he could harvest all his fields in one-quarter of the time.

The hand cranked grain cleaner which separates grain from chaff also has been widely adopted, with about one-third of the farmers using a small single-cylinder gasoline engine to turn the crankshaft, thus eliminating more backbreaking manual labor. Small motors of all kinds are an aid in a variety of operations, especially for pumping water for irrigation purposes in the river bottom areas.

Easily the most desired piece of machinery is the tractor, but only nine tractors are owned by farmers in El Pinar. In addition to its utility for pulling wagons, the tractor can be put to a multitude of jobs, such as pulling plows, harrowing, scraping, or clearing land, and as a stationary power plant for pumping water. However it is a rare farmer who can afford 225,000 pesetas for one of the cheaper tractors, and government subventions for tractors are given only to organized groups, not to individuals. Another limiting factor is that few farmers have enough land to make purchase of a tractor economically profitable. A few of the tractor owners do rent out their machines after they have completed their own farming chores, but again the high rental costs may keep a farmer from renting a tractor. In Leyes, there are several combines in use; these are owned by farm production cooperatives and are leased out to non-members on a per-hectare cost basis.

While tractors and combines are undeniably more efficient than hand labor, they are economical only when large areas of land are to be worked. Inasmuch as the *minifundio* conditions of the area still exist, it would be uneconomical for a farmer to purchase such machinery to work a mere seven or ten hectares of land.

There is other evidence of modernization of farm machinery in the area since about 1960. The traditional high-wheeled farm cart is gradually being replaced by a four wheeled cart which can be tractor drawn as well as mule drawn. Where farmers still use the two wheeled cart—and most still do—the wheels are automobile wheels mounted on an automobile axle instead of the iron shod wooden wheels of the past.

One of the most noteworthy characteristics of farming in El Pinar is the mixture of techniques representing the very old and the new, for example the use of a tractor to draw a threshing sledge. The sledge is virtually unchanged in style and construction since its introduction into Spain by the Romans; the tractor is, of course, a modern invention. Yet the two are hitched together and, regardless of the incongruity of the situation, a higher level of efficiency in threshing is achieved.

Livestock

Livestock in El Pinar can be divided into two basic categories: draft animals and animals for food usage.

The basic draft animal in the *comarca* is the mule. At one time oxen were the most common draft animals; certainly in 1949 oxen teams outnumbered mule teams in El Pinar. Today only one man in the village maintains a team of oxen. In the poorer villages, such as El Manzanal, they are seen more frequently. Indeed, one can use the relative presence of oxen to mules as a rough indicator of the prosperity of Castillian agricultural villages. (This would not hold true in the timber regions of the *Sierra* where a special large breed of oxen is used for hauling lumber up and down steep slopes.) Many burros are still seen although their number is declining. El Pinar has never had many horses; I saw only one—a wretched bony creature belonging to the blacksmith. By and large bicycles and motorcycles have replaced what few horses there were.

Sheep, once the wealth of Castile, have disappeared almost to the point of insignificance in El Pinar. In 1966 there were only four flocks totaling about 250 head in all. This is a far cry from the late 18th century in Segovia where enormous flocks of over 60,000 head were gathered together and driven through enormous buildings to be sheared for their wool. The sheep present today are sheared and some wool is sold, but mostly they are raised for meat, now a staple part of the villager's diet.

Pigs have been of major importance in this part of Spain for several centuries and almost every family keeps one or two swine in the family corral. When slaughtered, the pig provides the meat for the popular sausage, ever present on the family table. Salt cured hams are also very popular. Since there is very little wastage to a pig, it is one of the most important of all animals to the villagers.

Commercial swine raising began in El Pinar during the middle 1960's. These are feeder pig operations operated more by the industrialists than by the farmers. Many of the resin refinery operators established commerical swine herds as part of a diversification program and as a source of profit when resin prices fell off. One refinery was converted into a feeder pig yard and one major refiner began a large scale operation in 1967. Most of these swine are sold to the industrial meat packers in Segovia.

The swine currently most common in El Pinar is a mixed breed animal. However, a number of Landrace and Large-White swine were imported into Spain and the swine population is continually upgraded through selective breeding as well as improved feeding procedures.

Rabbits, once a common corral animal, were decimated by disease in the late 1950's and a few people now bother to raise them. In the days when meat was scarce, rabbit was the inevitable meat base for the family stew. Even the wild hares of the forest have decreased; in part this is due to the disease, in part to hunting, and in part to the clearing out of underbrush once common in the pine forest.

Chickens, like pigs, are a common corral animal; every family has a few chickens to supply them with eggs and which serve them as a meat supply. Yet, like the pig, chicken raising has become a major industry. Again, it is the industrialists more than the farmers who are engaged in full-time commercial scale broiler production. A number of broiler operations are located within the village, some in old refinery buildings. There are also two large egg producing operations. As with the swine, the eggs and broilers are sold to companies in Segovia although, to be sure, some local sales are made.

One herd of milk cattle is owned by a bar owner and kept in stalls near the Rio Grande bottom land. These are mostly low grade Holsteins, a few Jerseys, and Brown Swiss. The herd is T. B. and Brucelosis tested, but the milk is sold raw and unpasteurized. Milk is little used in the village except for babies, sick people, and to mix with coffee. However, housewives will boil the milk before using it. Milking is done by hand and the cows' udders are washed prior to milking. An effort is made to maintain sanitary conditions, but the dairy does not have either the equipment or trained personnel to do a fully adequate job. Mediterranean fever, carried by dairy products along the Levant and Andalusian coasts, is absent in the El Pinar area; fortunately bottled pasteurized milk is available for sale in two of the village's stores, being shipped in daily from the dairy co-operative in Segovia.

One large scale beef cattle operation started about 1964 and used a converted tobacco drying shed as a barn. Beef cattle raising is an innovation in El Pinar, although many farmers have traditionally kept one or two head for sale to the local butchers. The national government is trying to introduce large scale cattle raising into the area and has had some success with cattle cooperatives in villages to the east, but has met resistance in the El Pinar area. While the cattle may be let out to pasture, there is relatively little common pasture land in El Pinar. The cattle are kept usually in a feeder lot and given prepared feed instead of being allowed to graze.

Agricultural Extension Service

The agency that bears the major responsibility for improving the quality of Spanish agriculture is the *Servicio de Extensión Aqrária*—the Spanish equivalent of the American Cooperative Extension Service. The S. E. A. is a direct copy of the American Service and was first established in Spain in 1956. In 1966 there were 396 branch offices in operation and today there are over 500.

Agencies are located in *comarcas* which usually include from 10 to 20 villages each. In the El Pinar area, there are four agency offices: Villa Roman, Los Incierros, Fuentesol, and Villa Real. The agency in Villa Roman which services 14 villages. including El Pinar, has two agents. The offices in Villa Real and Fuentesol have more agents, but these *comarcas* are more dependent upon agriculture than El Pinar since they are not in the pine forest belt and have no resin industry.

Agents are never assigned to their own home towns, and generally not to any agency within 40 or 50 kilometers of it. Don Manuel, of the Villa Roman agency is from the province of Guadalajara. Don Francisco, the agent-in-charge is from another part of Segovia. Even though not assigned to their home towns, whenever possible agents are assigned to their native region. My assumption was that this was done because the agent would be familiar with the basic agriculture of the region, but Don Manuel was most emphatic in denying this. The reason is that the agent knows the *character of the people*. Spain has a variety of regional and sub-regional subcultures and one does not change agriculture until he first changes the farmer. And this cannot be done without a knowledge of people. Thus a Castillian is assigned to Castile, a Gallego to Galicia, a Basque to the *Vascongadas*, etc., whenever possible.

The *Agente Comarcal* (*comarca* Agent) receives generalized training in agriculture. Once assigned to an agency, he is expected to teach himself about the special crops grown in the area. An agent assigned to the Rioja area must learn about grapes since this is a wine producing region; an agent assigned to El Pinar must learn about wheat, barley and sugar beets, since these are the key crops. From time to time agents may attend short courses at one of the Service's training schools, but usually they learn by reading, direct observation, and experience.

The S. E. A. agent is one of the most respected persons in the village; his profession entitles him to the *Don* status but his clients are simple farmers and he must be able to communicate effectively with them. In addition to working directly with agriculturalists, the agent has to deal with the local power structure of each village in their *comarca*, know the local political situation inside out, and be able to converse with industrialists, bureaucrats, merchants, schoolteachers, priests, and the local police. I never met an agent who did not realize that successful human relations was his most important tool and weapon and that people came before plants in importance. These agents are not merely "playing a role" but are genuinely concerned with the welfare of their clients and of their towns. The farmers seem to recognize this also; after a short course in San Juan, the farmers gave both Don Manuel and Don Francisco a young lamb apiece as a token of thanks. When hardbitten farmers in a poor village do things like this, it is a sure sign of the effectiveness of the S. E. A. agents.

The agents use a variety of methods to get across their point. One of the most common is the use of the short course on a specific subject of local interest. Usually these courses are held during the winter months or sometimes during summer evenings—the time depending upon when most farmers can arrange to be present. The courses range from irrigation techniques, animal nutrition, soil conservation, and the like to occasionally more theoretically oriented material such as farm record keeping and business practices. In most cases the emphasis is upon practical application rather than upon abstract theory. Often the agents will give slide lectures or show motion pictures on agricultural topics. Attendance is usually good although in some villages, notably El Pinar, sometimes only ten farmers would show up.

The S. E. A. does not operate demonstration plots in the *comarca* although they have demonstration farms at Vallemonte, Alcala de Henares, Talavera de la Reina and other locations throughout Spain. If a farmer or group of farmers becomes sufficiently interested in a new crop or technique, the agents can arrange for him to visit one of these model farms. This is how tobacco was first introduced to the *comarca*; a local farmer passing through Talavera de la Reina saw the crop, asked questions, and then went to the S. E. A. agents for more aid.

To introduce a new technique, the agents set up demonstrations on land loaned by a local farmer. Seeds, tools, fertilizer, and other special equipment is procured by the agents either from their Service or from other government agencies, but the farmer must use his own land and do all the work himself. If the farmer wishes to adopt a new seed or requires some special equipment, the agents will act as intermediaries for him in his dealings with other agencies.

In the course of a normal day's work, Don Manuel and Don Francisco make a number of calls at farms, sometimes by invitation and sometimes just as an informal visit. Farmers often telephone or write the office for advice or come by personally. The average work day for the agent may begin at sunup and not end until late at night, and they work six days a week and sometimes on Sundays. In addition to the visits and courses, S. E. A. publishes a variety of literature written expressly for the farmer and given him free. The basic approach of the S. E. A. agents is to have the farmers discover for themselves the value of a new technique, and the only way to do this is by example. If a farmer sees that a new seed or a new fertilizer brings better results—either in higher crop yield or in a lesser work load for himself—he may well become an adopter.

S. E. A. agents are familiar with the American 4-H Club program and many *comarcas* have attempted to set up a similar program for village youth. The pioneer attempt in the *comarca* has been in the village of San Juan. Youngsters of both sexes have projects which they do independently of parental control. Meetings, excursions, award ceremonies, etc., are all part of the program and there is an international exchange program as well. During 1967 a young Missouri farm boy spent a month with a Spanish family on a farm near Peñafiel, in Valladolid province not far from El Pinar. No Segovian youth has yet been to the United States, but there is at least the hope for such a trip. However, the main value of the present program is in its attempt to teach the youth how to be better farmers and better citizens.

CHAPTER VI

Minifundio and Minipueblo

Land Reform

LANDHOLDING PATTERNS in Central Spain are basically *minifundio* in nature; that is, there is a proliferation of small plots of farm land as opposed to the *latifundio* system of large landed estates common in Andalusia and parts of Southwestern Spain.

In El Pinar, the average farm plot prior to 1963 was 0.3 hectares in size. The average farmer owned or rented twelve or thirteen such parcels, giving him a total land area of 3.7 hectares. The precise extent of *minifundio* holdings in El Pinar prior to parcel concentration can be shown with data provided by the *Servicio de Concentración Parcelaria* for the village.

The total land area of the village, excluding the actual village site, is 6,173 hectares. Of this area, 3,976 hectares are pine forests, 160 hectares are in common pasture land, and 22 hectares are meadowland not used for farming. Of the remaining 2,115 hectares available for crop cultivation, 1,846 are dry farmed, 30 are irrigated, and 239 are unworked inasmuch as they are sterile or otherwise unproductive.

Of the productive land, after exclusion of certain small plots of farm land that were devoted to non-agricultural usages (storage areas, cattle pens, etc.), 360 individual farm operators held between them 4,313 individual parcels totaling 1,320.4 hectares. If rented land is included, each cultivator had a total of 7.81 hectares. Considering alternate year rotation of fields, at best the average cultivator would work slightly less than 4 hectares of land.

Only 11 farmers owned plots totaling over 50 hectares. Sixty-nine farmers owned land plots ranging from 10 to 49.9 hectares, 30 farmers owned plots totaling from 5 to 9.9 hectares, and the vast majority, 133 farmers, owned plots containing 4.9 hectares or less. These are the so-called "postage stamp" plots characteristic of the *minifundio* landowning system. The basic characteristic of the land-holding patterns of the El Pinar area is that of miniscule plots, with the average farmer owning a few hectares and renting a few more.

Most of the land is held by farmers through inheritance, and the inheritance practices help account for the small holdings. Typically, a man with, for example, six children, will divide up his land holdings into six equal parts upon his death or retirement with each child receiving an equal share. Men and women both share alike; primogeniture is not practiced in the area. Thus, the typical farmer will own some land inherited from his father or mother and some which comes to him through his wife's inheritance. Often, he will be able to buy out one of his siblings and enlarge his own holdings.

Land in El Pinar has no sacred dimension; it is bought and sold and there is no mystical attachment of the peasant to his land. Land does represent wealth but buying and selling land is not an uncommon phenomena and has become more common as younger people leave farming as an occupation and move out of the village. However, most people prefer to rent out their lands to others instead of selling them since, as they say, one never can tell what the future will hold.

The average farmer, in addition to his own holdings, rents land from others. Pedro Gil's family, which lives in another region of Spain, owns over 250 hectares of land which they rent out to a number of farmers on a more or less permanent basis. Certain types of lease arrangements are protected by law; that is, the farmer has assurance that he will be able to lease the same land every year barring legally acceptable extenuating circumstances. The renter usually pays the owner a certain sum of cash based upon a percentage of the gross profit made from the land or a flat sum agreed upon by the two parties. In many cases the farmer works land belonging to non-farming kinfolk and shares the produce with them. This is often the case where the brother of a widow works her lands and shares some of the produce and profits with her.

Land values vary widely within the town limits, depending upon relative fertility, accessibility to water, distance from town, and a variety of other factors. Average land value in 1963 was 11,050 *pesetas* per hectare or 1.11 pesetas per square meter. In actual practice, when land was sold, it invariably brought a much higher price. The figures cited above were taken from government calculations and not actual sale prices.

The Parcel Concentration Service divided the land into nine categories and placed a price per hectare on each category as required by the re-parceling procedures set forth by law. River bottom plots were excluded since these were not subject to concentration; thus the prices refer mainly to plateau dry lands. The classes are numbered from 1 through 9 in order of value and priced as listed.

Class of land	Value per hectare
1	20,000 pesetas
2	18,500 "
3	16,000 "
4	13,000 "
5	10,000 "
6	8,000 "
7 (lands contiguous to the pine forest)	2,500 "
8 (barren clay soils)	500 "
9 (*Era* floors)	250 "

The Service was unable to provide specific figures on the number of hectares in each category. However, as has already been indicated, even the best land in the highest valued categories is the typical mediocre sandy loam of the area.

The law establishing the *Servicio de Concentración Parcelaria* and setting forth its goals and procedures was placed into effect in 1962. While concerned with the overall national welfare, the procedures take into account local sentiment and stress local initiative and participation.

A majority of the land owners of a village must request consolidation of parcels by petitioning their local municipal government. The petition, when approved by the village council, is forwarded to Madrid and the Ministry of Agriculture. The Council of Ministers—equivalent to the American Cabinet—approves the request and declares land concentration in the village area to be a matter of national interest. The matter then goes back to the Provincial level of the Service.

The land must be surveyed and all land records and deeds checked. It sounds simple, but the process of checking records and resolving disputes may take a year or more inasmuch as many peasants hold land without clear titles or land whose titles were destroyed during the Civil War when many public records were burned.

Once the legal spadework and the surveying is completed, new fields are laid out and allocations made. No person receives more land than he had originally, and if a person receives less, he must be compensated according to the value of the land he originally held. There is a period of time when the owners may dispute matters with the Service, but in actuality, relatively few disputes over allocation were raised. Most complaints were based upon the farmer's belief that he had received inferior lands or lands further away from the village than those previously owned. Jose-Maria Sanz Redondo's affidavit claiming that he was unhappy with the new land parcels he had received is typical. In a somewhat breathless run-on sentence he wrote the Engineer-In-Charge:

With reference to the judgement of the plots which have been given me, I am very unhappy and will yield to no one because I had a half hectare on the meadow which was for root crops and you gave me land in a clay area so goodbye sugar beets, chicory, watermelons, potatoes, (and) chickpeas, you tell me if I'm complaining out of spite; so I hope you'll rectify this because before I had it (land) three kilometers away and now it's five and I hope to hear favorable news from you because now I can't plant any of this.

Complaints were settled quickly and, all in all, only 4% of the land holders had a complaint of any nature to raise with the Service. A few of the villagers attempted to use their war service as justification for preferential treatment; a small number of "professional veterans" are found in every village and some of these complain about receiving poor plots while someone else who did not serve—or who was a "Red" —got a better deal. The policy and actual practice of the Service is to judge all cases strictly on merit and not pay attention to special pleadings or local politics. As a national agency, the Service is independent of local government or *caciques,* and thus able to neutralize attempts by local powers to influence plot allocations.[1]

Upon declaration of the land area of El Pinar as being of national interest on 28 March 1963, the Service began its efforts which were concluded in 1965. A number of parcels were excluded from the program, some river bottom areas as already mentioned, and some larger plots exceeding 7 hectares which were being or had been improved by the owners. The goal of the Service is to have minimum plots of 3 hectares each, although really effective dry farming would require a 30 hectare plot for maximum profit. After the exclusions of the above cited parcels, a total of 3,921 parcels was reduced to 544, each averaging 2.16 hectares or slightly below the desired average. Instead of each cultivator having 10 or 11 plots, he now had 3 or 4.

[1] An interesting account of land tenure systems and politics in Catalonia is given in Hansen, 1969:214-243.

At first, almost all the owners and cultivators complained, as Jose-Maria did, that they had received poor lands far away from the village, that the whole program had been bad for them, etc., but by 1967 they were all quite enthusiastic about the benefits wrought by the concentration. The rural sociologist in charge of the *comarca* noted that it usually takes about three years after completion of parcel concentration for the people to see the real benefits to themselves and to see that they had not been swindled, cheated, or otherwise abused. The *Concentración Parcelaria* program has been accepted by the people with a good deal of enthusiasm and the initial resistance to the program has diminished to virtual insignificance.

As a final precaution against the parcels being subdivided again upon the death of the owner, the law places severe restrictions that practically guarantee that the parcel will be indivisible except under very special cases, and even then, with approval of the competent legal authorities.

Comarca-wide planning

The parcel concentration program is being operated in close cooperation with other programs, especially that known as *Ordenación Rural*. This program is essentially a planning system which attempts to develop an entire *comarca* which is conceived as of a homogeneous social unit with similar socio-economic characteristics. The *Ordenación Rural* program in the El Pinar area is in its beginning stages and, indeed, in its beginning stages throughout Spain.

The major emphasis of the *Ordenación Rural* program is to upgrade the socio-economic status of the villages by effective long-range planning and help in coordinating activities of a variety of related governmental agencies at all levels. The major problem facing the planners is that of the very small village—the so-called *mini-pueblo* characteristic of central Spain.

Mini-pueblo is a neologism for the small agricultural village with insufficient resources to provide adequate levels of services such as electricity, sewerage, trash collection, medical services, etc. . . . The *mini-pueblo* is found in the *minifundio* area of Spain and is generally a village of less than 2,000 inhabitants. The figure of 2,000 is somewhat arbitrary but seems to be generally accepted as the minimum population a village must have to be economically viable.

The *minifundio* problem is generally broken down by planners into three major dimensions, all of which are interrelated:

1. The small size of the villages and their locations close to each other mean costly duplication of services, such as schools, administrative personnel, building upkeep, etc.

2. Small landholdings impede mechanization of agriculture and use of more efficient agricultural practices.

3. The level of living is so low that it is often described as being "infra-human." This violates the official ideals of social justice and human dignity supported by the State and the Church.

Every planning effort presupposes a supporting ideological base. Ideology consists of a way of interpreting phenomena. It is, as Bell and Kristol point out, "a preconception of reality" (1965:4). One of the sources of incongruity between the planners and the peasants is precisely that each has a different preconception of the realities of a given situation.

Basic to the whole *Ordenación Rural* program is an assumption that willful acts by the government are or can be directly responsible for change. This is certainly the assumption of the First Plan of Economic and Social Development in force during 1964-1967 and undoubtedly underlies all other change programs. There is a logical converse in that the lack of change—I should add favorable change—is due to bad government efforts or lack of efforts. Spanish sociologists were quick to point out:

What is certain is that, as we have seen, in Spain we have had very different rhythms of development within the same types of governments and, even, within the same government with similar administrators and ministers. For this reason, it should not be surprising that some may wonder if development is not to a certain point independent of one kind or another of political measures. (FOESSA, 1966:18)

An acceptance of this point of view obviously negates the value of planning and governmental efforts and, therefore, is nowhere officially accepted. When failures do occur or nothing gets done, a "victim" must be found. In Spain, the most common scapegoats are monopolists, bureaucrats, middle-men, or in the rural areas, the dumb peasants who won't accept progress when it is offered to them on a silver platter.

One of the most pervasive ideologies is the so-called Arcadian Myth. It is illustrated by governmental attempts to industrialize Spain without having peasants leave the farms. The rationalizations given to support the Arcadian Myth are many and varied, but their underlying rationale—if the term may be used here—is that the small towns, the *mini-pueblos,* are sort of a national "moral reserve," and their inhabitants are sort of Noble Savages living in an idyllic environment away from the vice and corruption of the city. Yet, I have heard planners at the administrative level refer to the peasants as a bunch of stupid clods, more stubborn than a Castillian mule, who live in filth and are perpetually involved in family squabbles and who rarely wash their ears. Admittedly, many see the inconsistency of the two points of view, but I cannot recall anyone seriously trying to reconcile the conflict.

Two classes of solutions are available to the *mini-pueblo* problem. The first is to move the people out to other places after first buying up their land. This has been done in some of the mountainous areas of Soria Province where land was taken over by the State Forest Patrimony for reforestation and conservation purposes. The second solution, which the government seems to favor, is to eliminate *mini-pueblos* as political units and have several of them merge with a nearby larger village which seems to be the most viable or offers the best prospects of development. In actual practice, the government uses the second *persuasive* approach insofar as is possible. The first mentioned *coercive* approach is a last resort and has, in fact, been used only once in Segovia when one village was to be flooded by a new hydroelectric project lake.

Once land concentration is accomplished, or well under way, the next phase is that of *Ordenación Rural,* meaning the orderly structuring of a rural area and synonymous here with a rural development scheme tied into a *comarca* wide program. The goal is to achieve maximum cooperative efforts among the farmers and other inhabitants. Efforts are made to have farmers combine plots and join together, with a government subsidy, to buy farm machinery. Technical training classes are given in farm machinery and related subjects by teams from the Ministry of Labor, while agents of the Agricultural Extension Service bring literature, lectures, and various types of aid to the farmers. Often new crops are introduced, such as tobacco in the El Pinar *comarca*. Since the government is trying to convert the Segovia plains area into a cattle producing zone, special incentives are offered to cattlemen or would-be cattlemen.

The initial success of the program has led Provincial authorities to the conclusion that the program should be intensified and extended throughout the entire Province. In a list of goals set forth for the new program, we see the death sentence for the *mini-pueblo*. Stated in the official terminology:

Give decided attention to rural nuclei of optimum dimensions so as to achieve through them the standard of living-comfort and services-desirable today.

The steps in the elimination of the *mini-pueblo* do not necessarily follow any set order but depend upon local conditions including the political influence of local industry, large landowners, and politicians. While farmers belong to the *Hermandad,* a sort of trade union and brotherhood, the top posts at provincial and national levels are well controlled by the government and the small farmer has very little real say in the major decisions.

One step is the concentration of municipal services and schools. Several villages are made to share one municipal secretary whose office would be in one of the larger towns. Many schools in small villages were closed and a central school established in the Villa Real *comarca.* These moves were not opposed too vigorously by the people although there was some grumbling about the distances children had to travel. However, school busses, a school lunch program, and the prospect of a better education for the children sufficed to eliminate serious objections. This concentration of services was being enthusiastically urged by the new Civil Governor of the Province almost from his appointment in 1968.

In some of the smaller villages, there is no longer a resident priest. A priest from a large village nearby comes to say Mass each Sunday and is on call in case of emergency. As priests are paid by the State, the presence of a priest in every hamlet was a serious drain on the economy.

Out-migration is both tacitly and openly encouraged by the government, although with some misgivings. Special courses are given to agricultural workers going to France and there is a French-Spanish accord on treatment of migrant workers designed to protect Spanish workers from possible abuse. While most workers plan to return to their village with savings, most of the younger ones eventually move permanently to the cities where better paying jobs await them. Government sponsored training courses in the villages seem to have the latent function of fostering migration. Most of these courses are directly related to local farming skills—tractor driving and maintenance, irrigation techniques, and the like. Yet, courses are devoted to brick masonry, plumbing and electrical installation and the number of graduates far exceeds the demand in the villages for such skills. A course in radio and TV repair held in one village of 600 inhabitants is a case in point; there are less than 200 television sets in the entire *comarca* and even a large village such as El Pinar cannot support a radio-TV repair shop. However, there is a future for electronics technicians in the cities.

The problem here is that planning must take a long-range view while the villagers are concerned with the immediate present. The incongruity of the situation is obvious; both peasants and planners realize that changes take time; where they differ is in their appraisal of the social costs of waiting that length of time. An example is a much discussed irrigation scheme which supposedly will be in effect by 1980 and which will undoubtedly improve crop yields in the El Pinar area. Few farmers can afford to wait until 1980, especially the younger ones who see more immediate opportunities elsewhere now. It was pointed out to me on a number of occasions that planners who concoct rural development schemes do not have to worry about crop failures affecting what will be on *their* supper plates.

At the present point—1969—*comarca* planning with regard to the *mini-pueblo* is in the *persuasive stage*. The techniques of change are education, upgrading of skills through special courses, concentration of lands and municipal services, and tacit encouragement of emigration from the area.

It is most unlikely that this alone will solve the *mini-pueblo* problem. Two forces will impede a large scale elimination of these small villages unless there is some drastic and unforeseen change in Spanish social and political structure. First, the Arcadian Myth grows stronger as rural depopulation continues and the cities become increasingly crowded. Each week newspapers report on the abandonment of entire *pueblos* with a tone of righteous indignation that such things should occur. Crowded conditions in Madrid and improved transportation facilities, including a large number of private cars, lead to a weekend exodus to the countryside and to the peaceful *pueblos*. Most city dwellers have family ties to some *pueblo* where they spend their summer vacations in an admittedly pleasant rustic environment and at low cost. With increased urban crime, juvenile delinquency, sexual promiscuity and decline in religious fervor in urban areas, the myth of the *pueblo* as the "moral reserve of the nation" is propagated, especially by intellectuals who, in turn, influence the planners but like them rarely venture out of the cities.

The second force is the resistance of the Castillian peasant who likes his home town and prefers to put up with substandard conditions (by urban reckoning) rather than move to a crowded city where he would be ill at ease. There is no necessarily "sacred" dimension to the *mini-pueblo;* most residents are quick to admit that living conditions are terrible, farming is a disaster, and life is often hard and brutal. For those who elect to stay there, it is simply their home town where they were born and where they expect to die. It is their village and if the government doesn't like it, that's too bad.

Again, we see the incongruity between the conceptions of the planners and the people. To the planners the *mini-pueblo* is a unit in a larger complex whole, generally an economic complex. It costs more to maintain than it produces; its level of living does not reach an "acceptable" national minimum, and it is socially and economically a burden on the nation. The villagers do not think of themselves as units of anything except of a family. To them the village is not part of a complex structure, but an independent world by itself with some ties to other little worlds around it and even more tenuous ties to something known as "the government" in Madrid.

If resistance to elimination becomes very serious, and if the government feels it is worth the social cost, the elimination can be done by *coercion*. A blueprint for such action exists in Segovia in a 1962 report prepared by the Economic Council of the Labor Union Organization which cites the traditional reasons why change has been slow in the area: peasant suspicions, ferocious individualism, unwillingness to give up old practices, ignorance, and so on.

The planners proposed a gradual strangulation of the *mini-pueblos;* 275 villages will be reduced to a total of 85. To urge the residents of the "condemned" *pueblos* to move out, it will be forbidden to erect new public buildings or make any but the most urgent repairs to existing ones. Roads will not be maintained at Provincial expense and only minimal expenditures for drinking water supplies will be permitted. All municipal employees paid by the national government will leave, schools will close, and government functions shifted to one of the main villages. In the 85 large villages selected for development, new housing areas will be opened for the resettlement of displaced villagers from the *mini-pueblos*.[2]

What the planners fail to realize is that interpueblo mobility is rare except in the case of marriage. The usual pattern is for the migrant to leave for a city rather than another village. The planners err in assuming community to be a purely physical and political entity and

[2] As of July 1970 • 31 pueblos, including 4 in the El Pinar *comarca*, had been administratively merged with larger *pueblos* in their vicinity. The villages themselves remain as residential and business centers, but are now political subdivisions of the larger *pueblos* to which they were annexed.

overlooking the network of social interactions that really is the heart of village life.

Spanish rural development planning is directed from the top down with little "grassroots" participation in the planning sessions; a situation which only widens the gap between the peasants and the planners perceptions of the situation. While there are rural sociologists in the planning agencies and at the applied action level, most have little training in empirical sociology and seem to have little influence on actual plans and procedures drawn up by technocrats in the Ministries.

Outmigration

As can be noted from the population pyramid in Figure 3 many villagers are absent six or more months a year from El Pinar. Most work in large cities such as Madrid or Bilbao or are on long-term contracts as farm laborers in France. Each year perhaps 50 to 75 young men and women from El Pinar go to France on a short-term basis as agricultural workers. They usually go for a two to three month period, although some have gone to pick grapes on a six-week contract.

Outmigration has always existed in Old Castile; historical reports indicate that depopulation has been a problem since the 11th century. The current wave began about 1960 when many of the industrialized European countries, France and Germany especially, were experiencing a shortage of workers. Spaniards prefer working in France since the cultures are reasonably similar and the language is not too difficult to learn. Some have gone to Germany and Holland to work in factories and, while pleased by high wages, were unhappy with the "cold" nature of the people they encountered. On many occasions in Switzerland, Germany, Holland, and France, I talked with Spanish workers. In general, most were pleased with the chance to earn high wages and to be able to send back a portion of their savings to their families. But, most said they longed for the day when they could return with enough money to establish a small business of their own in their native land.

The exact degree of influence exerted by returning migrant workers is hard to determine. Many, while in a foreign country, live in groups with other Spaniards and do not attempt to learn anything about the country they live in. Some of the young girls—those between 19 and 25 who work in France like the freedom women have in that country, but few dare demand the same degree of freedom in their home villages. Young men are charmed by French women but almost to a man state they would not marry one, preferring instead the "more moral" Spanish *señorita*.

Spaniards who work on French farms learn new techniques, especially in relation to the mechanization of sugar beet production. However, they are dubious that these methods can be used in Spain due to insufficient capitalization of the average *minifundio* farm operation. No major innovation in agriculture in El Pinar is attributable to emigrants who had spent time in foreign countries. What the foreign experiences do for the youth is show them that a more prosperous way of life exists and further show them that to achieve a better life, they need only leave the village for the areas where better jobs and higher wages are found.

Claudio Vela Prados and his wife Angelines are typical of the young emigrants from El Pinar. Next to the youngest son of a widow, Claudio followed his two older brothers' example and dropped out of school at about age 15 to work in Fausto's brickyard. His older brothers, Valeriano and Jose Luis worked at a variety of jobs in the village until they entered military service; upon discharge, they moved to Bilbao to work in a large factory. The youngest brother, Antonio, left El Pinar at the age of 17 to take a job as a welder's apprentice in the steel mills of Aviles on the Cantabrian coast. Their sister, Maria Teresa, until her marriage in 1968 to a local farmer, stayed at home helping her mother and going on two occasions as a migrant fruitpicker to France. The mother, Señora Carmen, lived on the pitiful 1,000 peseta monthly pension of her late husband and on whatever the children were able to give her. Since Valeriano and Jose Luis were married and had children, they gave little, and most of her support came from the younger children.

Angelines Olmos Gil, Claudio's wife, came from a more prosperous family of farmers and shopkeepers, but she too had dropped out of school to go several times to France to pick fruit. I first met her in a village near Carpintras in the Vaucluse region of France where I had stopped to see Claudio's sister Maria Teresa. The two girls from El Pinar were employed by a wily old Provençal farmer and were living, together with three other Spanish girls, in a converted garage. While the work, picking and packing fruit, was hard and the living conditions far from desirable, the girls were happy to be making much more money than they could have made in El Pinar or as maids in Madrid.

Claudio was 25 years old and Angelines 23 and they had been engaged for three years when I met them in 1966. They had to delay their marriage because they did not have sufficient money to build or

rent a house and furnish it; also, Claudio's job at the brickyard paid
only 90 pesetas a day which was not enough to support a family. In
desperation, Claudio quit his job at the brickyard and got a job in a
Michelin tire plant near Paris; later he was laid off and found another
job harvesting sugarbeets near Clermont-Ferrand.

Although both Claudio and Angelines sent money home to their
parents, somehow by living—existing would be a better word—on a
pittance they saved enough money to enable them to get married.
Only one obstacle stood in their way; Claudio had no job security in
France and neither did he have a secure job in Spain. Through the
efforts of a relative with political connections, Claudio obtained a job
in a government agency in Barcelona as a chauffeur. The pay was not
high, but it was a secure job and he normally had afternoons free.
Soon, he was able to get a part-time job driving a taxi.

After their marriage in January 1969, Claudio and Angelines rented
a small apartment in Barcelona for 3,500 *pesetas* a month. Consisting
of two bedrooms, living room, small kitchen, and bathroom, it is a
small and cramped place to live. Furnishings consist of a clothes closet,
double bed and chair in the bedroom; two easy chairs, a sofa and three
wooden chairs in the living room, and a small table and the normal
utensils in the kitchen which is equipped with a refrigerator and gas
stove. The second bedroom is used for storage and in it are hung two
hams and several strings of sausages brought from their familys' homes
in El Pinar. Their prize possession is a television set purchased on the
installment plan—a luxury they would never have afforded if they had
remained in the village.

Claudio earns a salary of 4,000 *pesetas* a month plus a month's
bonus normally accorded all government employees at Christmas and
on the 18th of July, which is the commemoration of the *Alzamiento
Nacional,* the Nationalist uprising which triggered the Civil War.
Since he receives a *per diem* when he goes out of the city, which is
often, his monthly salary usually amounts to 6,500 *pesetas*. Driving a
taxi brings in another 5,000 to 6,000 *pesetas* each month. Angelines
works as a seamstress from 8 A.M. to 5:30 P.M. each day and on Saturday mornings; her salary is based on piece-work rates and averages
about 7,000 *pesetas* a month. Together, all income included, the
young couple earns from 14,000 to 16,000 *pesetas* a month, a fantastic
salary by village standards. But Spain is in an inflationary cycle and
the cost of living is high in Barcelona—food, clothing, rent, and other
necessities are all much higher than in El Pinar. Together, they are
saving up to eventually buy an apartment (most apartments in Spain

are bought rather than rented) although they realize it may take five years until they can afford a decent apartment. They also want to wait at least three years before having any children since they don't feel that they can afford children (and the loss of Angelines' salary) at the present time.

An outgoing, friendly person, Claudio had no trouble adjusting to the Catalan population of Barcelona and, although Castillian Spanish is spoken everywhere, has learned enough Catalan to be able to converse with his fellow workers and taxi passengers. Angelines feels the Catalans—known widely as the most energetic and "European" ethnic group in Spain—are cold and is really ill at ease in Barcelona. She would much rather be back in the village near her family and friends. However, she is determined to make a successful life in the city. I helped Claudio and Angelines move into their apartment shortly after their wedding; Claudio had rented it without her having seen it, having left her in El Pinar while he went apartment hunting. She arrived as we were carrying in the big double bed, and the shock of the small bare apartment and the reality of life in an enormous and strange city was evident on her face; she looked like she wanted to cry. Six months later she was much happier, but it was clear that Barcelona, despite its advantages, was still very much of an alien world to her and would remain so for a long time.

Unlike many emigrants, Claudio has no desire to return to his village. "Why the hell should I starve there? Here, at least I can earn a living and not suffocate in a *pueblo* where there is never anything to do."

With Claudio's limited education, he and his wife realize that he will never rise much above his chauffeur's position, but with effort and in time they can achieve a respectable income and perhaps a lower-middle class life far above what would have been possible in El Pinar. While many emigrants speak longingly of the day they can take their savings and return to the *pueblo* to buy land or open a shop, few ever do return for more than a visit. The *pueblos* are dying and the emigrant who has seen the greener pastures of the cities knows it, and once having left his birthplace, he finds he cannot bring himself to go home again.

Claudio and Angelines are among the lucky ones, but for every man like him, there are perhaps 5 others who never get jobs paying more than 4,000 *pesetas* a month digging ditches or acting as bricklayer's helpers, or—in the case of women—being maids at an even lower salary.

The reaction of the Spanish government to emigration abroad has been divided. On one hand, emigration is favored because the emigrants usually send home money and thus help the nation get hard foreign currency. Emigrants also stay out of overcrowded Spanish cities which have more people than jobs. On the other hand, there is a fear that the emigrants will return with new and dangerous ideas about the nature of government and the Church. Those who attend the short courses given to prospective emigrants are cautioned about these dangers. In the notebook of one young man who had attended the short course in Segovia was a printed speech by the course director warning the men of the dangers of losing their faith and of being ensnared by false democracies—i.e., forms of government ideologies in conflict with that of the national Regime. But those who return with little faith are those who left with little in the first place. Likewise, those with the most articulate anti-government sentiments are the intellectuals and urban based groups, not rural villagers.

The depth of the desire for a better life is reflected in a survey by the *Sindicatos* organization in Segovia. A random sample of villages was selected and all agricultural entrepreneurs interviewed—the sample is representative of the rural farm population of the province. (SSE, 1964:49-50)

Two sets of figures are of relevance here:

(1) Divided by age groups, the following percentages of individuals wish to change from farming to another occupation.

a.	under 15 years	26.3%
b.	from 15 to 24 years	39.98%
c.	from 25 to 64 years	14.27%
d.	over 64 years	0.00%
e.	total of all individuals	19.52%

(2) Divided by age groups, the following percentages of individuals wish to migrate from the villages.

a.	under 15 years	74.87%
b.	from 15 to 24 years	69.35%
c.	from 25 to 64 years	21.65%
d.	over 64 years	0.00%
e.	total of all individuals	31.43%

If a further subdivision in age categories were made in the 25 to 64 age group to set up a group from 25 to 40, the percentage of this group would be equivalent to the 15 to 24 year olds. In any case, the figures are clear—the youth want out.

While it is reasonable to expect that returning emigrants could be effective (or at least active) change agents, what happens is that most of them return to the village only to leave again, and then, to stay away. In effect, what the emigrants—permanent and temporal—bring to El Pinar is not so much new ways but the word that new and better ways exist and to achieve them one must leave the village. Youth leave seeking a better life, and the old people stay for there is no place else they know and they are resigned to their fate. Even those farmers who are successful wish to leave, but many are trapped by a lack of skills or by family obligations and remain to till the soil and hope for better days.

Whenever possible, many of the emigrants return to the village in August—the normal month for vacations—and during the week-long fiesta in June. During these periods they show off their new clothes, and in a few cases, their automobiles, and all this serves to stimulate more youth to leave the village. The village is crowded, and a good many merchants make a large proportion of their annual income during these relatively brief periods. Food often becomes hard to obtain and prices go up as merchants cash in on the opportunity. Many of the returnees spend freely in the bars, and this helps the local economy. But El Pinar has only one small boarding house and gets few tourists except for city dwellers who will come to spend a Sunday afternoon by the rivers. Villa Roman does attract some tourists and has a hotel of sorts as does Leyes. But these tourists are Spaniards on low budgets and contribute little either in the way of innovative ideas or financial enrichment for the villages.

CHAPTER VII

Values and Change

MANY STUDIES OF peasant societies note that village social life goes on in a context of envy, mutual distrust, and conflict. Daily life and social interaction is characterized, overtly or covertly, by mutual suspicions and the general expectation of brittle social relations. The conflict is intra-village; it covers conflicting social relations between groups and individuals within the community. Foster (1960-61:174-176) cites numerous examples of conflict situations in many peasant communities and indicates that this phenomenon is more or less typical of peasant societies in general.

Lopreato studied a southern Italian village and stated that "the peasants of Stefanconi are given to suspicion, quarrels, vituperation, abuse, violence and conflict of all sorts" (1961:586). Foster found the same type of situation in Tzintzuntzan, Mexico (1948). Lewis, in his study of Tepoztlan (1951), also noted the presence of conflict and related phenomena.

The studies of Spain by Pitt-Rivers (1954), Kenny (1961) and Lison-Tolesano (1966) do not emphasize conflict, although Pitt-Rivers does note the distrust of the peasants toward outsiders, the resentment against the rich, and the importance of gossip in the community. Lison-Tolesano's work is more historically oriented, but the nature of conflict is clearly expressed, especially intra-familial conflicts.

Amoral Familism

E. C. Banfield in his *The Moral Basis Of A Backward Society* (1958) describes life in Montegrano, a poverty stricken southern Italian village. He cites the envy and hostility present and notes that attempts at cooperative activities—including political activities—designed to promote community welfare never succeed nor even get off to a decent start. Silverman (1965), Friedman (1953) and the novelist Barzini (1964) cite similar evidence from other Italian villages.

Banfield, in attempting to explain the phenomena, coined the unfortunate phrase "amoral familism" to denote a worldview which the villagers *seem to be following*. The basic postulate of amoral familism is:

Maximize the material, short-run advantages of the nuclear family; assume that all others will do likewise.

The postulate is a hypothesized worldview reflecting the fact that the family is the primary reference group for the peasant. From the basic statement, Banfield draws a corollary which states:

In a society of amoral familists, no one will further the interests of the group or community except as it is to his private advantage to do so.

The value of these hypotheses, as Banfield points out, does not depend upon the possibility of showing that any or all of the people *consciously* follow the rule, but rather its value is demonstrated if the people act *as if* they follow it. However, any statement of values abstracted by an anthropologist should be intelligible to the people. Finding evidence of amoral familism in El Pinar, I cited some of Banfield's concepts to various people without revealing the source and learned that in most cases people did in fact think this way. The postulated worldview Banfield set forth is empirically verified by the statements and actions of the villagers of El Pinar, at least to the extent that the hypothesized world-view serves as a good explanation of their behavior.

The *as if* criterion stated above is defensible on the grounds that people are often not consciously aware of why they do certain things, or why they tend to follow a certain course of action. Worldview is practically impossible to measure directly; at best we can get an approximation of what the person is thinking by *post hoc* analysis of his behavior.

Banfield's ideas have not lacked criticism. Cancian (1961) and two Italian scholars, Pizzorno (1966) and Marselli (1963) attacked it on both logical and historical grounds. A Dutch scholar, Wichers (1963) rebutted the arguments of Pizzorno and Marselli and stated that he had evidence to support the hypothesized worldview from studies of rural Holland.

Banfield proposed a number of predictive hypotheses derived from his basic statement of amoral familism. A number of these are not directly relevant to El Pinar, inasmuch as the political systems of Spain and Italy are different, but nevertheless most of them are applicable.

The first hypothesis is that no one will further the interests of the community unless it is to his private advantage to do so. This is substantiated in El Pinar, and in other villages of the *comarca*. One of the major criticisms leveled by the people against the Moreno family was that they did nothing to help the community. Yet, during the years when Eusibio Moreno was the *cacique,* he did sponsor a number of actions for improving roads and some physical facilities. These actions were interpreted by the people as actions designed to benefit Moreno primarily—better roads made it easier for his trucks, and so on.

When the village physician served as Mayor he built a house for himself out of public funds. This was quite legal inasmuch as each village must provide housing for the resident physician. Yet, he was criticized severely for his actions just as he was for instigating the drying up of a few ponds which served as breeding places for insects. The construction of the new clinic was criticized by many because they felt it was primarily for the benefit of the doctor and the *practicante*. In no case did people accept altruism or a desire for community betterment as a motive for action by others. This substantiates the second hypothesis offered by Banfield: "Claims of any person to be motivated by zeal for the public good rather than private gain are regarded as fraud."

While the village of Villa Roman has an ambitious Mayor and an equally ambitious City Council, these men are constantly suspect. It is undeniable that the village has been transformed from virtual ruins in 1949 to a very pretty and well developed place today, but the means by which some of the officials have also prospered lead the people to wonder just how much zeal for the public really figured in their actions. Similar cases can be reported for other villages in the *comarca*. In San Juan a wealthy woman, born in the village but living elsewhere, offered to build a swimming pool free of charge if the village authorities would provide a piece of land. The land in question was useless clay soil of no agricultural value. Title to the land would remain with the village and the title to the pool would also revert to it upon completion. The villagers were divided in their opinion of the project and ultimately refused permission to build the pool. No one, they felt, would make such an offer unless there was some catch to it. They were unwilling to accept the woman's explanation that she was acting out of charitable motives—it was really asking too much of them to accept such a statement at face value.

Banfield offers seven related hypotheses about peasant reactions to political office and officeholders. These are:

1. Officials only concern themselves with public affairs for which they are paid. Private citizens' interest in public affairs is regarded as abnormal and even improper.

2. Few checks are made on officials by the people; only other officials do the checking.

3. Office holders do only the minimum necessary work to maintain themselves in office or to get promoted. Professional and educated people generally lack a sense of mission or calling. High positions are regarded by their holders as weapons to be used against others for their own private advantage.

4. Officials take bribes when possible and are assumed by the people to do so even when, in fact, they do not.

5. There is no connection between abstract political principle and concrete behavior in ordinary daily life.

6. The ballot is used to obtain the greatest short-run gain.

7. It is assumed that politicians and elected officials are corrupt; this assumption is made as soon as the official takes office. The tendency in electing officials is to vote against someone rather than for some person.

We may deal with the hypotheses in a more integrated framework. Generally speaking, officials restrict themselves to their areas of competence only and will not act if they feel that their actions infringe upon the areas of another official's duties. In part, this is normal behavior as regards jurisdiction. It is also a way of avoiding decisions or of "passing the buck." This behavior is most noticeable at the Provincial level where things seem to take forever to be decided. A Spanish proverb says *"Los asuntos del palacio van despacio"*—affairs of the palace go slowly.

Most City Council meetings, in El Pinar as in most places in the world, have few members of the general public in attendance. Except during the *resinero* crisis of 1967, I was usually the only visitor in the session even though the meetings are open to the general public. People are concerned with activities of the Council only if those activities directly affect them. If a citizen gets too inquisitive or intrudes too much into municipal affairs, it is thought to be improper not only by the authorities but by the general public, since his interest is probably motivated by desire for some private gain.

As can be seen from the history of the controversy between El Pinar and Villa Roman over *Communidad* profits, officials are checked only by other officials. Only in cases of great public scandal will the public demand an accounting of an official's behavior. To otherwise try to check is to run the risk of incurring the wrath of some functionary and that, of course, means troubles and the loss of tranquility.

It is true that most office holders do only the bare minimum necessary to keep their jobs or to get promoted, but certain groups of officers must be exempted from this claim and indeed are by the people. The same holds true for many of the professionals and educated people. Clearly, in El Pinar, most of the schoolteachers are highly motivated to do a good job. The Agricultural Extension and P.P.O. workers are virtual missionaries at their jobs—and these are positions where promotions are slow in coming and are usually based upon seniority rather than ability. Don Jaime, the *practicante* of El Pinar, was one of the very few in El Pinar genuinely concerned with improving the lives of the young people. In this case, his zeal was recognized by the villagers who elected him to the Village Council by a vote almost double that achieved by the other candidates together. Yet when he tried to have Provincial authorities pave a section of the main road which has long been in execrable condition, he was criticized by the villagers on the grounds that since his house was on the road, he was looking out for his own welfare first.

Village level authorities have little power and thus it is difficult for them to use their positions as weapons against their enemies because their machinations would be immediately visible for all to see and criticize. Generally, the authorities of El Pinar are honest and not corrupt. However, there have been decisions, such as the one that allowed Paco Ruiz, a farmer and friend of a City Hall clerk, to build a house in an area where new construction was forbidden by the village's zoning plan, which raise questions in the minds of the people. There is a little bribery in El Pinar, but more often than not officials will grant special privileges or overlook improprieties because of friendship or kinship ties and not because they are paid off. Other questionable cases come to mind, especially in Villa Roman. For example, how did "El Duro" arrange to get a scholarship for his little girl when other parents were unable to obtain application blanks supposedly available at the City Hall? How did a former Mayor accumulate enough money to build a block of apartment houses on his small salary as a clerk in a refinery and without a large inheritance? Since the average villager is inclined to think the worse of his fellow man, especially when they hold posts of authority, he is quick to suspect bribery and dishonesty although he will rarely discuss his thoughts for fear of reprisals against him.

The use of the ballot in Spain is limited. Mayors are appointed by the Provincial Governor who is in turn appointed by the Head of State. The only elected officials are the city councilmen. Men are elected on the basis of personality and popularity, although a large number of voters consider other merits of the man. Merit usually means what the person will do for the voter and his interests. It is assumed that the office holder will be looking out for his own special interests or those of his employer or patron, but as long as the man in the street sees a chance of getting something for himself, he does not care too much about any possible corruption, since he doesn't expect his officials to be very honest. Many people said that, if elected or appointed, they would probably do the same things that they criticized others for doing or allegedly doing.

The connection between abstract political ideology and actual daily practice is remote. Promises by the State, the Church, as well as by the critics of the Regime are regarded by the villagers as so much hot air. All agree that the stated ideals are fine; they just wonder when they will be put into practice. This is not a criticism leveled at the Regime —most of the *comarca* is pro-Franco and he is respected although not universally beloved. The villagers distrust any government—Republican, Monarchy, or what have you. However, the activities of the S.E.A., the P.P.O. and similar agencies have given the peasant some hope for the future and some tangible evidence that "Madrid" does in fact care for their welfare.

Another hypothesis states that the weak favor a regime which will maintain order with a strong hand. This is quite true in the El Pinar area. The Franco Regime has had its share of critics from within and from without Spain. After the Civil War order was restored with a rough hand; there were political prisoners jailed and many executed. Things are much more open and liberal today, although political efforts against the Regime are usually crushed with quick efficiency by the police. Newspapers and magazines are censored but not as blatantly as before. Political parties other than the *Falange* are prohibited and political meetings other than those sponsored by the regime are prohibited as well.

The villagers—peasants and professionals alike—are agreed that they are "a hard people to govern." They see the need for a government strong enough to force them into unity. They say that the average Spaniard is like a mule; he will not move unless threatened with a stick. The average peasant expects an authoritarian regime and even desires one, although he will not tolerate a dictatorship or a repressive tyranny.

The villagers are the weak people of Spain just as the villagers of Banfield's Montegrano are representatives of the weak of Italy. His hypothesis stands confirmed in principle, as can be seen above and by the people's conception of the "ideal leader" discussed earlier. The last of Banfield's hypotheses of relevance states that gains accruing to the community are valued only by the person if he benefits from them. He will reject measures to benefit the community if he receives no personal benefit, considering himself worse off if his neighbors' positions increase for the better while he gains nothing—even though he also loses nothing. No amoral familist ever thinks he gets a fair share. This concept has been more fully developed by George Foster in his 1965 article "Peasant Society and the Image of Limited Good" and merits further attention.

Limited Good

The concept of Limited Good is simply that the peasant sees his world—the village and its natural resources—as having or containing a finite amount of "good." This quantity is divided up among the villagers and cannot be expanded. The good may be tangible property such as land, or it may be intangible such as a set of rights.

The improvement of one man's position can be achieved only by depriving another, since the amount of good is finite and limited. This view seems to imply a sort of relative deprivation concept, and is not limited to Spain, Italy, or the Mediterranean area. Foster does not limit the presence of this attitude to peasant societies exclusively; it is common in developing nations and may well be present to some extent in industrialized societies.

The only way a person can advance himself without being suspected of depriving his neighbors is to be lucky, for example, winning the soccer pool or holding a winning number in the lottery. If the source of the benefit comes from outside the village through, for example, the aid of a patron who gets a person a well paying job, this too is permissable since the "good" comes from what is conceived to be another "world."

Foster's concepts go well together with Banfield's and the two theoretical models overlap in many aspects. The people of El Pinar act as if there is a limited amount of good, especially land and money. Where cooperative efforts are attempted, they act as amoral familists.

Worldview and Resistance to Change

The emphasis on being honorable, the need to avoid shame, the ties that bind a person to his family, the pressures of religious beliefs, and the fear of the ¿que diran? are factors which inhibit the Castillian villager and which in turn impede his acceptance of certain changes. Until recently El Pinar and thousands of villages like it were tightly closed little worlds in which there was usually only one acceptable way of behaving and one way of seeing the world. To live a decent life, the villager had to share in the view of the world of his fellows or, if he could not, then he had to escape to some other place where more freedom of choice existed. But today the mass communications media combined with easily accessible transportation and improved education have changed the situation dramatically. The rural development plans now in effect have followed on the heels of a general opening up of the rural society, and the villager is caught in between the old ways and the new.

Robin Horton (1967) in contrasting African magical thought and Western science uses the idea of open versus closed societies. The degree of openness of the society is dependent upon the number of alternatives available to the people at a given moment. Greater choice among alternatives is equivalent to a more open society: modernization is essentially a process of ever expanding alternative definitions of situations and modes of response as more alternative explanations become available.

Yet the availability of large numbers of alternative responses is not sufficient in itself to allow us to expect less resistance to change or a higher rate of adoption of innovations. In a provocative treatment of the anthropology of evil, Arden King (1968) claims that the opening up of new alternative modes of explanation may be the source of great trouble. It is his contention that the point at which knowledge has increased sufficiently to force the people into a conscious examination of their basic values and world view is also the point at which "evil" appears.

The implications of this argument on the problem of explaining resistance to change are significant as departures from structural approaches where the ecostructure or the economy determined the subsequent behavioral responses and where worldview was ignored or relegated to a position of relative unimportance.

The use of the conceptions of "open" and "closed" societies as outlined by Horton are useful since they do not depend entirely upon economic variables. The presence or absence of alternative modes of explanation in a society or the relative strength or weakness of alternative modes, where present, provides a clear conception for distinguishing the role of values in a change process. (Furthermore, Horton's conceptual framework allows for an analysis of the peoples' view of their history, while typologies such as Redfield's "folk-urban" do not.)

The people of the El Pinar *comarca* have accepted certain of the planned changes willingly and often eagerly. Specifically, they accepted new wheat and barley seed, tobacco, sugar beets, new irrigation techniques, mechanized farm equipment, new conservation measures, and the use of the *pico a corteza* resination process. Technical courses taught by the *Promoción Profesional Obrela* and *Servicio de Extensión Agraria* have been received with general enthusiasm.

A good deal of resistance was shown toward the land consolidation program directed by the *Servicio de Concentración Parcelaria*, but the resistance in central Spain has died down now that other villages have seen the success of the initial pilot projects, some of which took place in the vicinity of El Pinar.

Real resistance has been shown to the establishment of farm production cooperatives in which members would pool their land and efforts in order to buy government subsidized machinery with which they could more efficiently cultivate and harvest crops. While a few of these were in operation in *comarca* villages, all were characterized by a high degree of internal dissention and most of the members wanted to disband the groups but were impeded from doing so by law.

Changes most readily accepted are those of immediate and direct benefit to the individual and his family. Changes most readily resisted or rejected are those which force him into long-term contractual relationships with his fellows, long-term being anything over ten days or two weeks according to local reckoning. A number of attempts to set up farm production cooperatives in the *comarca* have failed simply because farmers felt uncomfortable as members of a formal association which bound them to other farmers by a complex set of rules and regulations. Manolo, one of the best farmers in the village, refused to join a cooperative because he did not wish to be bound by decisions made by others and also because he saw no immediate economic benefit in it.

Significantly, the goals of the cooperative efforts are not rejected. What are rejected are the *means* of achieving those goals. Economic profit, however desirable, is subordinated to social considerations. In brief, the social costs involved make cooperation too expensive.

The Castillian peasant frequently views his world as a place where trouble lurks at every turn; a world of suspicions and mistrust where order is a tenuous thing difficult to achieve and more difficult to maintain. To be sure, he is friendly, gregarious, and free to offer help on a short-term basis without thinking of payment. Yet the fear of disorder, disharmony and trouble is ever present and the signs are everywhere abundant: the barred windows, the secrecy that pervades business deals, and the ever-present fear of the ubiquitous "they" who seem to be so powerful an agent of social control.

Explanations of resistance to change often focus upon apathy as a causal variable, thus leading many researchers to look for the root causes of such apathy. Peasants are supposedly apathetic because they are poor, because they are ignorant and/or illiterate, because they distrust authority which has done little but exploit them, because of class antagonisms, or because of beliefs inherent in religious codes such as Islam or, in the Spanish case, traditional Roman Catholicism (*cf.* Niehoff and Anderson, 1966).

Apathy is not a good explanation for resistance to change or a necessary cause for failure to adopt an innovation. If a person refuses to participate in a change program, it may well be because he prefers some other mode of action, including his traditional one. Behavior labelled as apathy is better conceived of as a response to a situation stimulated by the prevailing values and beliefs of the society. In this way, apathy is not doing nothing; rather, it represents an active choice among alternatives that, granting his worldview, are perfectly logical to the peasant. When planners refer to peasants as apathetic, oftentimes what they really mean is that the peasant is not interested in something *they* think he *should be*.

Castillian peasants' closest ties and primary loyalties are to the family and not to the village. That his efforts are mainly directed toward the welfare of that family should surprise no one. This is not to say that he is unaware of, or unconcerned with, community welfare; rather, he sees community welfare as properly being the concern of the village officials. Except in the most dire periods of crisis, he does not involve himself with officialdom for that is a good way to get into trouble, and trouble is at the root of village social roles and interactive behavior.

I have stressed the high value placed upon tranquility, which is to say, the absence of troubles. Much of the resistance to social innovations can be understood as being responses to situations that pose a threat to tranquility. In a community where inter-familial conflict is prevalent, where one man's gain may be another man's loss, and where each man is expected to look after his own family's interests first, he has all the troubles he needs without going out and volunteering for more.

The formal organizations with which the villagers are familiar tend to be dominated from the "outside," that is, the Church or the State. While he may respect these bodies, the villager also knows that they have tended to exploit him in the past and may still be doing so. When these organizations try to get him to cooperate and share with others, they do not realize that the peasant sees the world in different terms and, as long as the concept of limited good is prevalent, he will resist out of fear of being deprived of what little he has or for fear that some neighbor will gain some good and thus upset the delicate balance in the distribution of goods that already exists. If we add to this complex the value placed upon individuality, we see that value conflicts are often at the root of resistance. To the urban dweller and intellectually oriented planners and administrators, this resistance appears foolish and is attributed to either apathy, stupidity, or rampant *egoismo*. Since peasants are supposed to act like this—according to the learned ones in the city—no one is surprised when development plans fail, nor does anyone search for any new explanation of why the plan may have failed.

It is apparent that planned change programs brought in by "outside" agencies may be regarded as a threat by the peasant. If it is a simple matter of a new technology, the resistance can be overcome without too much difficulty. However, when changes are introduced that depend upon the creation of *new forms of social relationships as a necessary condition* for the change, strong resistance occurs.

Joining a cooperative is viewed by planners as a logical step in the upgrading of agricultural productivity which will eventually pay dividends to both the peasant and to the State. To the peasant, however, long-term cooperative membership in a formal association is viewed as a denial of what little freedom of individual action he has left to him as well as an invitation to trouble. He sees himself becoming involved in the affairs of others and their becoming involved in his. This is all the more true because he will be formally linked to individuals whom he may not trust in serious affairs and may well have to take orders from one of these people who assumes a leadership role in the cooperative's hierarchy.

Granted the social structure and value orientations of the village, it is unreasonable to assume that the villager—who sees himself as individualistic—will delegate part of the control over his livelihood and property to other individualists whom he cannot trust to do with them as he might do. The average villager realizes that much of his individualism is only an illusory and highly problematical potential which can never be realized as overt behavior. Membership in a cooperative may be a surrender of a portion of this cherished illusion—the ability to do what one wishes with ones' own things. If this cognitive orientation exists, and the data indicate it does, then we may have a good model which explains at least part of the resistance to change programs requiring cooperative efforts.

To be individualistic means that the villager may exhibit behavior of such a type as to get him involved in controversy with others, and that, of course, may mean getting into trouble. The conflict of value orientations is evident: by actualizing or attempting to actualize this potential to do as he pleases, he must run the risk of getting involved in an unpleasant mess. The course of action actually followed in the *comarca* is oriented toward the maintenance of harmony by avoiding actions that would of necessity involve others in your affairs and vice-versa. I suggest this as a more fruitful approach than the tiresome historical explanation that Castillian countrymen are the way they are because of inertia, ignorance or lack of opportunity. These latter explanations do not hold very well for Castile in the last fifteen years nor do they come to grips with the fact that El Pinar and eighty-five other pine-forest based villages in Segovia have had a very high literacy rate and a relatively high level of living since at least 1900.

Joining a cooperative is running the risk of a loss of tranquility. It is to put oneself into a secondary or business relationship with others with whom one has had only primary personal relations. The village social structure has no adequate normative base for this situation nor any idea of the role requirements of a member of a formal, complex, and task-oriented association. Unlike the Andalusian situation, where cooperation and association is found in regards to water rights, no such tradition exists in the El Pinar area. El Pinar and its *comarca*—and, I suspect a large part of the cereal growing area of Old Castile—simply feels that the social costs of joining a cooperative outweigh the economic advantages.

The conflict in value-orientations described here makes more sense when we view the village as a residual category whose "function" is to control conflict and regulate the units comprising it—the units in this case being families. Any number of studies confirm the fact that new situations may bring about suspicion, mistrust and fear. Furthermore, the degree of inter-personal and inter-familial hostility in Spanish villages is great; a phenomena common enough in peasant villages throughout the world.

Examined in the light of the value system of the village, even the best of "ideal leaders" would be hard put to operate effectively For one thing, it is hard to see how they would develop in a village where no opportunity for development exists. Elected officials on the village council are not taken seriously by the people. The socialization of the child provides him with few experiences where he can elect leaders—both the structures of the Church and the schools are hierarchical and highly authoritarian. If an "ideal leader" could be found, he would have to come in from the "outside," i.e., from the city, and this would create other problems.

If membership in a long-term cooperative program involves, as I think it does, a high degree of ego-involvement by the villager and the fear of loss of both tranquility and individuality, then resistance to joining is logical and expectable.

When a villager can be persuaded to join, any weakness in the internal operation of the cooperative will bring forth violent emotional reactions by the villager who now sees his own worst fears being confirmed. In the cases I have observed, the upset and distraught villager immediately blames himself for having joined and blames his fellow members for having caused the trouble the group is in. The legal organization of most cooperatives is designed to keep members in for a certain number of years, usually six since cooperatives must amortize debts and pay off government subsidies. Now hopelessly welded to the group, tranquility ceases to exist and life becomes one big lio. At this point no leader is to be trusted. If the leader is a local person, he is abused for his stupidity, ineptness, etc. If he comes from the "outside," this reinforces the villagers' view that the government—any government—is interested in the farmers only to exploit them.

Thus, even the orders of the "ideal leader," if indeed he gives any, are circumvented, ignored, or as in the famous Spanish phrase: obeyed but not complied with. The "ideal leader" in these situations is almost useless and may even wind up being the scapegoat unless conditions improve rapidly.

One of the significant social characteristics of the El Pinar area is the decreasing importance of certain traditional integrative patterns. The Patron-Client relationship described in Spain by Kenny (1959) and still strong in Latin-America hardly exists in El Pinar. The Church has lost much of its power to control the people and even the traditional village-wide events of a sacred dimension have lost much of their meaning. *Cofradias* have little importance. Membership in the farmer's *Hermandad* or in one of the government controlled trade unions is taken for granted and these bodies bring people together but do not unify them.

When the villagers say that they don't know how to cooperate with each other, they are quite right. What is lacking in El Pinar is a set of norms defining such long-term contractual relationships among a large group of people, say from about seven or eight on up. The only long-term and enduring group that the people know is their family. In periods of crisis or necessity the family can be quickly mobilized to produce immediate results and benefits even if these are, as Banfield notes, short-run benefits. Granted the empirically demonstrable fragility of inter-personal and inter-familial social relations in the villages—whatever their historical or psychological origins may be—Banfield's hypothetical worldview seems most logical.

In effect, the introduction of social and even technological innovations depends greatly upon the indigenous systems of social control which are so closely inter-related and mutually reinforcing. Inter-familial and inter-personal long-term cooperation is not deprecated by the people; rather, they see themselves as being incapable of achieving it. In contemporary El Pinar, "amoral familism" seems to be a behavioral state which allows people to maintain tranquility, a semblance of individualism and self-autonomy, as well as public order—all at the same time. Until new norms and roles are evolved allowing for the creation of contractual, instrumental, non kin-based associations which can operate effectively on a long-term basis, agricultural reform and rural development plans of any significance will be either blocked completely through resistance or else be unable to operate effectively because of internal dissentions.

Postscript

THE RECEPTION AT the hotel was a warm one; Señor Aceves the American anthropologist and steady customer was back again. "Going back to that *pueblo*?" asked the concierge, "Well you better hurry up and finish your book because it won't be here the next time you come." Pepe's comment was meant only half in jest; he knew as well as most Spaniards that the waves of emigration from farm villages were as a church bell signalling a death, in this case the death of a village. Sometimes the deaths are dramatic: an entire village in Avila is offered for rent by its inhabitants who have fled to the cities; a *pueblo* in Valladolid once the home of 500 people lies abandoned like some Nevada ghost town. What then is the future of El Pinar? A slow death?

The economic realities can be stated simply: the income from the pines is no longer sufficient to allow the village to provide necessary services to the people, and farming of cereal grains is neither sufficiently attractive nor remunerative as an occupation to hold the young people in the village. The social realities can be stated with equal simplicity: improved education plus widespread use of radio, television and printed material enables the villager to learn more about the "outside world" and exposes him to new alternatives which frequently appear to be more attractive than the old ways. The title of the old song, "How're Ya Gonna Keep 'Em Down On The Farm After They've Seen Paree" aptly, and sometimes literally, describes one of the major problems of the mini-pueblo. Except for the old people who have nowhere to go and a few farmers with sufficient land to earn a decent profit, most of the people under 40 would like to leave the village. Many cannot, but their children usually can and do.

Much of the future of El Pinar and villages like it will depend upon factors over which the villagers have little or no control. The Food and Agricultural Organization of the United Nations has recommended to the Spanish government that it close resination of pines in Segovia and begin to tap the faster growing trees in the Galicia region of Northwest Spain. If this recommendation is followed, some 7,000 *resineros* in Old Castile will be out of work, and other jobs will be hard to find in an economy already plagued with unemployment. The Ministry of Agriculture is attempting to work out a plan by which the farmers in the El Pinar area will give up growing cereal grains and go into cattle raising, so as to both cut down on annual wheat and barley surplusses which cannot be used or exported and ease the balance of payments problem by cutting imports of beef needed to feed the country. Spain, like most developing countries, is caught in a situation whereby as it develops its cities and industries more meat and less bread is consumed.

Other factors will also affect El Pinar. How long will countries like Germany and France continue to have a labor shortage and thus provide work for Spaniards? When some large German factories laid off, temporarily as it turned out, many foreign workers in 1967, there was consternation in Madrid. Not only was a source of hard currency threatened, but where would these Spanish workers find jobs if they returned home? How long can the present tourist boom last? A decline in tourism can mean unemployment for thousands of Spaniards working in the hotel and allied industries. Then there is the greatest unanswered question: will there be a stable government after Generallisimo Franco passes on?

Returning to the village level, there is an obvious need for the development of new norms and attitudes which will allow the people to engage in large-scale, long-term cooperative ventures such as the farm and cattle raising cooperatives essential for a more productive agriculture. The day of the small *minifundio* farm operation is virtually gone in Spain and only those with large-scale rational exploitations of the land will be able to live well. Whether the various government agencies working under the Second Plan of Social and Economic Development currently in force will be successful in changing attitudes of the villagers is something we shall have to wait and see.

The villager grows up and is socialized in a culture that stresses hierarchy and obedience to superiors. By custom and law the father is the head of the family to whom the wife and children must defer. Despite some liberalization, village priests still tend to stress obedience and subordination to God's will as it is interpreted by the Church hierarchy. Village schoolteachers still stress rote memorization of facts and strict obedience to the teacher's will. While villagers are not always pleased with having to submit, they are used to it, and many, when they reach a position of superiority, will use that position to dominate others just as they have been dominated in the past.

How then can it be expected of these people to participate in the democratic procedures designed, for example, by government planners for the operation of cooperatives? How then can they be expected to place their trust in a leader when the very concept of leadership is imbued with the idea of domination which all find unpalatable unless they themselves happen to be elected or appointed to that status?

The problem of El Pinar illustrates the truism, pointed out by Ogburn in his theory of "cultural lag," that social changes take much longer to be accepted than technological changes. For the people of El Pinar, the new alternatives will not be of any use until some of the older norms are changed or done away with, a process that they have come to realize is not necessarily as simple as it sounds. However, judging by the way they have adopted some of the changes—technological and social—discussed in this book, El Pinar may well adapt and survive.

My last visit to El Pinar was in July 1970, shortly before this book went to press. The situation in the village was little changed from the description I have given here. A few more people have cars and television sets, there is some increase in mechanized agricultural techniques, and the young people are still leaving their homes for a new and better life elsewhere. Salaries have risen above levels cited here, but inflation has continued to eliminate any major gains in real income. While a bitterly cold winter froze much of the cereal crop, there was a slight rise in resin prices and the village economy remains relatively stable.

Despite Pepe's worry that El Pinar might not be there when I returned, it was. For reasons I cannot explain, my feeling is that, while its decline is certain, it will never entirely disappear but will, somehow, endure.

References Cited

Banco Español de Credito (cited as BANESTO) 1966 *Anuario del Mercado Español.* (Madrid).

Barzini, Luigi 1964 *The Italians.* (New York: Atheneum).

Bell, Daniel and I. Kristol 1965 "What Is The Public Interest?", *The Public Interest,* No. 1.

Cancian, Frank 1961 "The Southern Italian Peasant: World View and Political Behavior," *Anthropological Quarterly,* vol. 34.

Caritas Española 1965 *Plan C.C.B.,* vol. 1. (Madrid: Euramerica S.A.).

Collins, Larry and D. Lapierre 1968 *Or I'll Dress You In Mourning.* (New York: Simon and Shuster, Inc.).

Comision Superior de Ordenación Urbana de Segovia 1955 *Plan de Ordenación de ("El Pinar"), Memoria Descriptiva.* (Segovia). .

Foster, George 1948 *Empire's Children: The People Of Tzintzuntzan,* Institute of Social Anthropology Publication No. 6. (Mexico, D.F.: Smithsonian Institution). 1960-61 "Interpersonal Relations In Peasant Society," *Human Organization,* vol. 19, No. 4 (winter). 1965 "Peasant Society and the Image of Limited Good," *American Anthropologist,* vol. 67, No. 2 (April).

Friedman, F.G. 1953 "The World of 'La Miseria,'" *Community Development Review,* vol. X. (1958) originally printed in *Partisan Review,* 1953.

Fundación FOESSA 1966 *Informe Sociológico Sobre La Situación Social de España.* (Madrid: Euramerica S.A.).

Gonzalez Casanova, Francisco 1948 Mss. of a speech to the Centro Segoviano de Madrid on the history of the Communidades of Segovia.

Hansen, Edward C. 1969 "The State and Land Tenure Conflicts in Rural Catalonia," *Anthropological Quarterly,* vol. 42, No. 3, (July).

Horton, Robin 1967 "African Traditional Thought and Western Science —Part II," *Africa,* vol. 37, No. 2, (April).

Kenny, Michael 1959 "Patterns of Patronage In Spain," *Anthropological Quarterly,* vol. 33 1961 *A Spanish Tapestry: Town and Country In Old Castile.* (London: Cohen and West). 1961-62 "Social Values and Health In Spain: Some Preliminary Considerations," *Human Organization,* vol. 21, No. 4, (winter). 1965 "Poise and Counterpoise in the Presentation of the Spanish Self," *Anthropological Linguistics,* vol. 7, No. 4.

King, Arden 1968 "The Anthropology of Evii," paper presented at the Annual Meeting of the Southern Anthropological Society, Gainesville, Florida, March 1967.

Lewis, Oscar 1951 *Life In A Mexican Village: Tepoztlán Restudied.* (Urbana: University of Illinois Press).

Linz, Juan and Amando de Miguel 1966 "Within-Nation Differences and Comparisons: The Eight Spains," in R.L. Merritt and S. Rokkan, eds., *Comparing Nations: The Use Of Quantitative Data In Cross-Cultural Research.* (New Haven: Yale University Press).

Lison-Tolesano, Carmelo 1966 *Belmonte de los Caballeros.* (Oxford: Clarendon Press).

Lopreato, Joseph 1961 "Social Classes In An Italian Farm Village," *Rural Sociology,* vol. 26.

Marselli, G.A. 1963 "American Sociologists and Italian Peasant Society: with reference to the book of Banfield," *Sociologica Ruralis,* vol. 3, No. 4.

Niehoff, A.H. and J.C. Anderson 1966 "Peasant Fatalism and Socio-Economic Innovation," *Human Organization,* vol. 25, No. 4.

Peristiany, J.G., editor 1966 *Honour and Shame: The Values of Mediterranean Society.* (Chicago: University of Chicago Press).

Pitt-Rivers, Julian A. 1954 *People Of The Sierra.* (New York: Criterion Books). 1963 *Mediterranean Countrymen.* (Paris: Mounton & Cie.).

Pizzorno, Alessandro 1966 "Amoral Familism and Historical Marginality," *Community Development,* (new series), vol. 15-16.

Price, R. and S. Price 1966 "Noviazgo In An Andalusian Pueblo," *Southwestern Journal of Anthropology,* vol. 22, No. 3.

Servicio Sindical de Estadística de Segovia (cited as SSE) 1964 *Productividad Y Empleo Agrário: Una Investigación en la Provincia de Segovia.* (Segovia).

Silverman, S.F. 1965 "Patronage and Community-Nation Relationships in Central Italy," *Ethnology,* vol. 4, No. 2.

Wichers, A.J. 1964 "Amoral Familism Reconsidered," *Sociologica Ruralis,* vol. 4, No. 4.

Suggestions for Further Reading

Collins, Larry and D. Lapierre 1968 *Or I'll Dress You In Mourning*. (New York: Simon and Shuster, Inc.). This popular account of idol matador "El Cordobes" gives a vivid and realistic account of poverty in rural Spain and a deft description of social conditions that help drive young people out of the villages.

Douglass, William 1969 *Death In Murelaga*. (Seattle: University of Washington Press). A detailed study of funeral customs among the Basques that illustrates the social structure of the people.

Kenny, Michael 1961 *A Spanish Tapestry: Town and Country In Old Castile*. (London: Cohen and West). A comparative ethnography of a mountain village and a working class parish in Madrid.

Lison-Tolesano, Carmelo 1966 *Belmonte de los Caballeros*. (Oxford: Clarendon Press). An ethnographic and ethnohistorial account of a village in the Province of Zaragoza written by Spanish anthropologist.

Michener, James 1968 *Iberia*. (New York: Random House). A general description of Spain and Spaniards by a famous novelist, this is perhaps the best recent book of its kind on the country.

Pitt-Rivers, Julian A. 1954 *People Of The Sierra*. (New York: Criterion Books). A now classic account of life in an Andalusian pueblo by a noted British social anthropologist.

+++++

For readers fluent in Spanish, there are a number of excellent works by Spanish authors which are well worth reading, such as:

Anlló Vazquez, Juan 1966 *Estructura Y Problemas Del Campo Español*. (Madrid: Editorial Cuadernos Para El Dialogo). A detailed account of the problems facing the Spanish agriculturalist and the small rural villages.

Delibes, Miguel 1950 *El Camino*. (Barcelona: Ediciones Destino). Written by one of Spain's foremost novelists and journalists, this short novel deals with a young boy growing up in a small village. Delibes, unlike many Spanish intellectuals, knows and cares for the people of the pueblos and transmits his feeling in this excellent book.

Escobar, Julio 1966 *Se Vende El Campo*. (Madrid: Afrodisio Aguado S.A.). Set in a rural village near the El Pinar area, this novel traces the effects of emigration on two farm families accurately and sympathetically.

Perez-Diaz, Victor 1966 *Estructura Social Del Campo Y Exodo Rural*. (Madrid: Editorial Tecnos S.A.). A sociological study of a village in New Castile and the problems stemming from emigration.

Index

Glossary

Agente Comarcal   District Agent of the Agricultural Extension Service; like a County Agent in the U.S.

Alcaldia   The office of the Mayor (the Mayor is called the *Alcalde*)

Alzamiento Nacional   National Uprising; the term used by the government to denote the beginning of the Civil War on July 18, 1936, when Franco and his supporters began the overthrow of the Second Republic

Ano y vez   Alternate year rotation of crops and fields

Arriba   A Madrid daily newspaper

Auto de fe   "Act of Faith" usually involving the execution of religious deviates during the Spanish Inquisition

Bachiller Elemental   Grammer school diploma or graduate

Bachiller Superior   High school diploma or graduate

Barrio   Neighborhood

Beatas   Sarcastic term used to denote those (usually old women) whose major social life revolves around church attendance at Masses, Rosaries, etc.

Becerrada   An informal bullfight involving young bulls or wild cows who are "fought" by village youth or by anyone wishing to get into the ring. A mock bullfight

Bodega   A wine cellar

Cabezudos   A person wearing a large papier-mache head which covers his body. He accompanies the *gigantes* during the fiesta celebration

Cabra   Female goat

Cabritos   Little goat, diminutive form of the noun *cabra* (goat)

Cabron   Literally, a large male goat, but implying that a man is a cuckold. This is the worst possible insult that can be given a man

Cacique   A politically/economically important person whose influence dominates a community although he might not hold any formal office

Capataces, Capataz   Title of a skilled worker who is usually in charge of some special task as roads or forests. He acts as a sort of foreman over workers

Centimos   Cents, the smallest unit of currency, 100 centimos = 1 peseta

Ciguenal   Device for taking water from a well using a long counterbalanced pole to which a rope and bucket are attached

Chato   A "short drink," slang expression for such a drink, usually wine and soda

Clases Medias   Middle class

Cocido   Stew, usually made of meat, potatoes, and chick peas

Cofradias   Catholic brotherhoods and confraternities, usually devoted to the veneration of a particular saint

Comarca District

Communidad "Commonwealth"—a multi village association for common use of lands belonging to several villages as a whole

Corridas Bullfights

Cuartel Barracks

Diputacion Provincial Provincal Assembly or legislative body

Distrito Forestal Forest District

Don, Dona Honorific title

Duena Chaperone

Egoismo Selfishness, self-centeredness

El Adelantado de Segovia Daily newspaper of the Province of Segovia

Era Threshing floor

Falange The Falangist Party (Falange means Phalanx) which supported Franco and which has been, in great part, subsumed into the *Movimiento Nacional*

Fiesta Feast Day or Festival, usually in honor of a saint or with other religious basis

Formal Dignified

Frente de Juventudes Government sponsored youth group which is part of the Falange Party with activities similar to U.S. Boy Scouts. This organization was renamed to *Organizacion Juvenil Espanola* with essentially the same activities and purposes

Gallegos People from the Galacia region of Spain

Gigantes A stilt walker dressed in costume who walks around during the fiesta

Gloria Literally, "glory," but referring to a heating system for houses using an exterior fire pit with tunnels under the floor to carry the heat to the rooms

Guardia Civil Civil Guard, a para-military police force primarily active in rural areas of Spain but controlled by the national government

Hermandad "Brotherhood," actually a form of labor for agriculturalists

Hijas de Maria The Daughters of (the Virgin) Mary—a womans religious sodality

Hogar Literally meaning fireplace. The term is also used to mean a home

Hombria Manliness

Instituto Laboral Special school for training workers for skilled jobs

Jefe Local del Movimiento Local chief of the "National Movement"—the only legal political party in Spain. Usually the mayor of the community is assigned this post

Jota Spanish folk dance

Jubilados Retired persons

Latifundio Large scale landholding system common in southern and western Spain

Lios Troubles

Lugares Places, usually referring to human settlements

Machismo Masculinity expressed by repeated sexual adventures, seductions, etc.

Meseta The tableland, i.e., the plateau areas of Old and New Castile

Meterse en lios To "get into a mess"

Minifundio Small scale agricultural operations and landholdings

Mini-pueblo See text for definition

Ministerio de Gobernación Home Ministry responsible for local governments

Municipios Municipalities

Mus A Spanish card game

Noche de Sabado A Saturday night television variety show

Noria Water well using an animal to turn a machine that lifts buckets of water from the well

Ordenación Rural An agency responsible for rural development programs

Padron Municipal Civil Register of a municipality containing vital statistics

Pariente Relative, kinsman

Pasadoble A dance but usually used to refer to spirited music played during bullfights

Paseo Promenade or stroll

Personalismo Personalism, the attitude of putting one's self ahead of all others

Pesetas Basic currency unit of Spain. 1970 value is 70 pesetas to $1.00

Pico a Corteza The technique of extracting pine gum by use of an acid solution placed in the cut made by resineros

Pinus Pinaster Latin name for the resinous pine found in central Spain

Plan de Ordenación Plan of development

Practicante Physician's assistant and male midwife

Promocion Professional Obrera Government Agency which trains workers in new skills, both for industry and for agriculture

Pueblo (1) a village (2) the people

Resinero Pine tree chipper, one who works extracting resinous gum from the trees

Señor, Señorito Señor = Mister; (señorito explained in text)

Serenos Night watchman

Serio Serious

Servicio de Concentración Parcelaria Government agency whose mission is to concentrate farmers' small land plots into fewer but larger plots

Servicio National de Cereales National Cereals Service—government agency which buys grain from farmers and aids in maintaining price supports from the commodity

Siesta A nap usually during the afternoon

Simpatico Friendly, agreeable, sympathetic

Sindicato Trade union

Sin Verguenza Shameless, usually applied to women although not exclusively

Típico Typical

Toreros Bullfighters

Tranquilidad   Tranquility

Tute   A Spanish card game vaguely like whist

Uve   Literally, the letter "u." This describes the "u" shaped cut in the pine made by the resinero to extract the raw gum from the tree

Vecinos Cabezas de Familias   Family head, usually male, who in certain elections is the only member of his family allowed to vote

Vendimia   Grape harvest

Vino   Wine